IN
WICKLOW
WEST KERRY
and
CONNEMARA

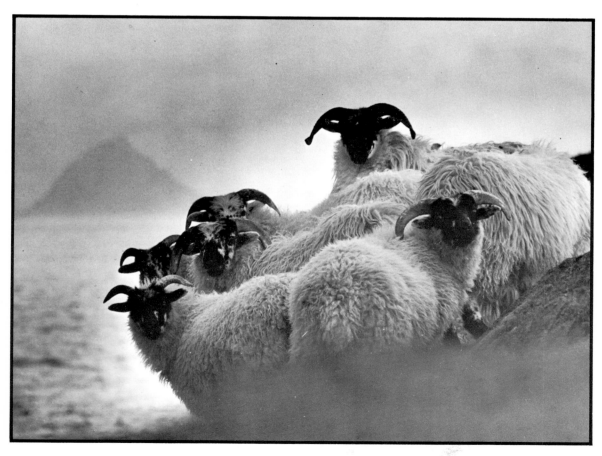

1. Great Blaskei Island

2

IN
WICKLOW
WEST KERRY
and
CONNEMARA

by

J. M. SYNGE

essays by

George Gmelch and Ann Saddlemyer

photography

George Gmelch

ROWMAN AND LITTLEFIELD
TOTOWA, NEW JERSEY

First published 1980
The O'Brien Press Ltd.
11 Clare Street Dublin 2

First published in the
United States 1980 by
Rowman and Littlefield, Totowa N.J.

ISBN 0 8476 6260 8

Jacket design – Sharon Gmelch
Book design – Michael O'Brien and Sharon Gmelch
Typesetting and layout – Redsetter Ltd.
Printing – E. & T. O'Brien Ltd., Dublin
Binding – John F. Newman Ltd., Dublin

2. *Jug and Hand-basin*

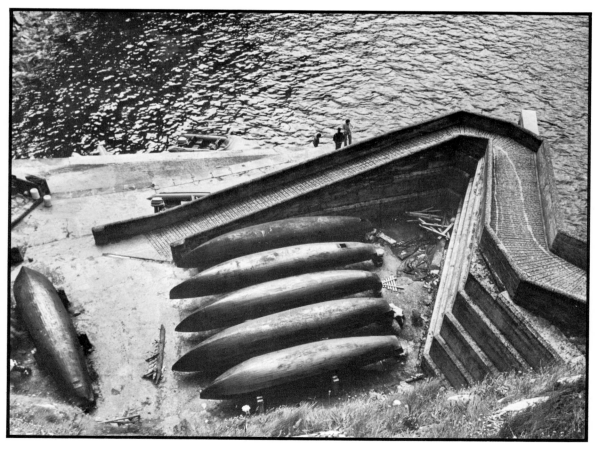

3. Naomhóg, Dunquin

Contents

Preface

This book contains fourteen essays written by J. M. Synge around the turn of the century. The book is divided into three sections: *In Wicklow, In West Kerry* and *In Connemara.* Most of the essays were originally published in the *Manchester Guardian* and in *The Shanachie,* an Irish literary magazine published quarterly in the early 1900s. The essays were first collected and published as a book in 1910, the year after Synge's death. The publisher Maunsel and Co. of Dublin reprinted the book several times in the following decade. It then went out of print until 1966 when it appeared as part of the Oxford University Press four-volume collection of Synge's work. In this edition we have made a number of additions, including two introductory essays, an index and about fifty photographs. The first essay describes Synge's experiences among Irish country people and highlights features of his background and personality which help us to understand his writings on peasant life. In the next essay Ann Saddlemyer examines the importance of *In Wicklow, West Kerry and Connemara* as the source material for Synge's plays.

The photographs, taken especially for this edition, provide images of the subjects and places Synge describes. The landscape of rural Ireland has changed a great deal since Synge's time with tarmacadam roads replacing rough tracks, land reclamation and enlargement of farms, afforestation projects, and modern bungalows with pebble-dash walls and manufactured tile roofs appearing where white-washed, thatch cottages once stood. The people have not remained unchanged either — the motor car, bus service, radio and television and most recently membership in the E.E.C. have brought them, even in the remote parts of the West, into the modern world. While some of the simplicity of their traditional ways is still in evidence, they are no longer peasants. Despite such changes the photographs also show that much of the splendour and charm of the countryside described by Synge remains. The areas — Wicklow, west Kerry, Connemara and northern Mayo — are still the most beautiful spots in Ireland.

The photographs in this edition were taken in the summer of 1978 and in February 1979 when all of the places Synge describes were visited. Two 35mm cameras were used, a Nikon and a Nikkormat, with four lens ranging from 28mm to 200mm. The films used were Kodak's Plus-X and Tri-X.

In putting together this edition I received the generous help of many people. I am especially grateful to Sharon Gmelch, my wife and colleague, and publisher Michael O'Brien for their valuable suggestions and criticisms throughout. I am indebted to Pat Langan for his perceptive comments on the photographs. I thank Peter Thursfield for sound advice on printing and Harry Kolker, Tom Donnelly and Peter Mooney for their excellent darkroom work. I must also acknowledge Edna Gmelch and Gary Geiger who over the years have taught me most of what I know about photography. To my good friends Margaret and Vincent Jones who live in Synge's birthplace at Newtown Villas in Rathfarnham, I owe my first interest in Synge's writings. Tom and Josephine Murphy made excellent suggestions on the captions and Paddy Dunleavey provided information about Great Blasket Island, his former home. Mrs. Lily Stephens kindly gave permission to reproduce the photograph of Synge. Joan Somich typed the essays. Others who assisted in various ways were Don Bennett, Dave Simms and Eithne Russell. Finally I wish to thank the staffs of the National Library, the library of University College Dublin, and the manuscript room at Trinity College Library for their helpful assistance.

George Gmelch, Dublin, March 1979

J. M. Synge with his family

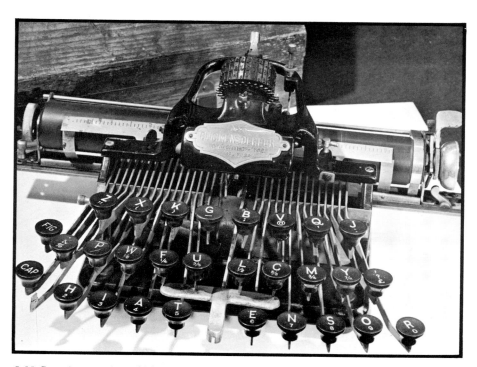

J. M. Synge's typewriter which is preserved in Trinity College, Dublin

10

J. M. SYNGE
Observer of Irish Peasant Life
George Gmelch

As a young man, solitary and introspective, Synge immersed himself in the study of
natural history. He took frequent long walks through the woods near his home in
Rathfarnham where he would lie in the bushes and watch the movements of birds.
Darwin's *Origin of the Species,* which he read at the age of fourteen, led him to
doubt and later reject his family's strong religious beliefs. About this period in his
life he later wrote, 'My studies showed me the force of what I read, [and] the more
I put it from me the more it rushed back with new instances and power. Till then I
had never doubted and never conceived that a sane and wise man or boy could
doubt. I had of course heard of atheists but as vague monsters that I was unable to
realise . . . My memory does not record how I returned home nor how long my
misery lasted. I only know that I got the book out of the house as soon as possible
and kept it out of sight, saying to myself logically enough that I was not yet
sufficiently advanced in science to weight his arguments, so I would do better to
reserve his work for future study. In a few weeks or days I regained my composure,
but this was the beginning. Soon afterwards I turned my attention to works of
Christian evidence, reading them at first with pleasure, soon with doubt, and at last
in some cases with derision . . . By the time I was sixteen or seventeen I had
renounced Christianity . . . The story is easily told, but it was a terrible experience.
By it I laid a chasm between my present and my past and between myself and my
kindred and friends. Till I was twenty-three I never met or at least knew a man or
woman who shared my opinions.'[1] Independent and free thinking, Synge in later
life was also to reject the landlordism and British allegiance of his ascendancy background.[2]

During his summer vacations at the family residence in Co. Wicklow, Synge
turned his curiosity to the people of the countryside.[3] He enjoyed the company
of countryfolk, their spontaneity and wild sense of humour were a welcome escape
from the polite formality of his class. On the roadside he stopped and chatted with
tramps, and wrote down their stories and odd phrases of speech in his notebooks.
In later years he spent many summers among the people of western Ireland,
especially on the Aran and Blasket Islands. As the anthropologist does today, he
participated in the lives and activities of the people he observed, recording their

work, their pleasures and their outlooks on life. In writing, Synge's aim was not to present mere factual information on the customs of Irish peasant society but to give insight into the consciousness of the people. And this he did better than any writer of his time.

The people he describes in these essays were among the most traditional in western Europe at the time. They were also among the poorest. Half the population in western Ireland lived on farms of less than 15 acres and about 15 percent had fewer than 5 acres.[4] The mixed cottage farming economy in which farmers had a few plots of potatoes and oats, poultry, a pig and a few cows or sheep produced barely enough for subsistence. A bad year, severe frost, too little or too much rain-fall, could produce hunger and even starvation. The Great Famine (1845 - 48) in which more than 1 million Irish people died of starvation and 1½ million fled the country was still within living memory. In Connemara and northern Mayo the small plots of land worked by families did not yield enough to meet their subsistence needs. So farmers also fished, harvested and sold kelp, and cut turf which they sold to the inhabitants of the stony off-shore islands who had no bogland of their own. In Mayo only seasonal migration to Scotland and England for work as farm labourers kept families from pauperism. But in all parts of Ireland, west and east, peasants also depended upon the remittances they received from their emigrant offspring to make it through the year.

The acute land shortage which had forced people to abandon the pre-famine custom of subdividing the land among all the sons in a family and adopt inheritance by only one child was in the process of bringing about a major transformation in the rural social structure. In a dramatic reversal, the Irish peasantry changed from being one of the earliest marrying peoples to the latest and most frequently celibate people in Europe.[5] Between 1845 and 1914 the average age of marriage for men rose from 25 to 33, the average female age from 21 to 28, while roughly one-quarter of both sexes never married at all. The change in inheritance patterns required by land consolidation condemned a family's younger children to the emigrant ship or celibacy. By the turn of the century emigration had become a fact of life which touched almost every rural family. Though all parents understood its necessity, watching their children leave was never an easy thing to do. As Synge observed, 'At one place an old woman was seized with such passion of regret, when she saw her daughters moving from her, that she made a wild rush after the train ... I could see her writhing and struggling on the platform, with her hair over her face, and two men holding her by the arms' (p. 98). By 1901 the population of western Ireland had dropped to just 43 percent of its pre-famine level.[6] Though economic conditions in the east improved considerably from the turn of the century onwards, the poverty and emigration from the region during Synge's time was not markedly different from that of the west.

Though Synge's main concern was with the lifeways of the people, he was also sensitive to the landscape. He believed that the personality of a people is strongly linked to the mood of the place in which they live. Synge did not describe the scenery in minute detail, rather he attempted to capture its essence and mood. The physical setting of the three regions Synge visited are very different in character. Wicklow is mountainous — it comprises the largest area of continuous high ground in Ireland. Its beauty however lies less in its peaks than in the glens and wooded valleys which cut deeply into the rolling dome-like hills. Wicklow's reputation as the 'Garden of Ireland' comes largely from the splendid deciduous woodlands which cover much of the valley floors and mantel the hillsides. In places such as Glendalough, Glendasan and Glenmacnass streams cascade from the central massif of the Wicklow mountains into the valleys forming elegant waterfalls. Compared with its overwhelming dominance in most of Atlantic Ireland, the coastline is of little consequence in Wicklow. It is relatively straight, with long stretches of unbroken and unspectacular cliffs which make the sea inaccessible in most places. In large measure the people of Wicklow have turned their backs on the sea. There are few significant harbours. Pride in their landscape is rooted in the beautiful wooded glens.

In west Kerry one always senses the presence of the sea.[7] Its hilly peninsulas provide most of the inhabitants with a vista of the Atlantic. Unlike the gentle and somewhat uniform Wicklow coastline, Kerry's is rugged with long tongues of rocky land reaching out into the Atlantic swell. And unlike Wicklow, trees are scarce, in places virtually non-existent. Because of the salt spray and direct exposure to Atlantic gales, trees grow only in a few spots where the mountains offer protection. Thick fuschia hedges which line the lanes and roads are west Kerry's most characteristic vegetation. Around the deep bays between Kerry's three large peninsulas (Beara, Iveragh and Dingle) sandy beaches such as the magnificent strand of Inch alternate with steep rocky cliffs. The mountains of west Kerry rise abruptly from sea level to more than 3,000 feet. They are the highest and most spectacular in Ireland. Unlike mountains elsewhere in Ireland, the summits in west Kerry especially those on the Dingle Peninsula stood above the glacial ice sheets which scoured the surrounding landscape and rounded off other mountain tops. Below the summits there are U-shaped valleys and hanging lakes, characteristic features of glaciation. Completely treeless, exposed and capped in clouds, the peaks have the appearance of being even taller than they are.

The landscape of Connemara is less dramatic but no less picturesque. The dominant image of Connemara is of bog and lake-covered lowlands set against the Twelve Bens, a group of quartzite peaks about 2,000 feet high. It is a land of muted colours in which violets, ochres, blues, greys and multi-hued greens mix together in kaleidoscopic combinations. The inhabitants of Connemara are densely settled in small compact family farms along the coast, leaving the interior virtually isolated. The coast is carpeted in granite boulders, and the numerous stone walls built by the inhabitants appear to enclose little more than boulders. In Synge's words, 'the fields looked so small and rocky that the very thought of tillage in them seemed like the freak of an eccentric' (p. 116).

There is a fourth area which Synge visited and describes in several essays in Part Three and that is north-western Mayo, particularly the peninsula of the Mullet and Blacksod Bay. This is one of Ireland's most desolate landscapes, much of it vast areas of bogland and very little of it suitable for cultivation. Synge considered the district 'the poorest in the whole of Ireland' (p. 143). On the Mullet Peninsula the land can be thought of as three long strips running north to south.[8] The first strip, on the Atlantic shore, is formed by a magnificent white strand and extensive sand dunes in the process of migrating inland. Next, in the shelter of the dunes lies the only cultivable land. It supports tiny plots of potatoes and oats. This narrow strip of soil, however, quickly gives way to the third zone — the acidic and poorly drained clays of the Blacksod coast which are suitable only for rough grazing. Reflecting the longitudinal zoning of the soil, the townlands have been divided into narrow east-west bands to give everyone a fair share of what little good soil exists. Across the bay and within view lies the most extensive bog in the country.

When the time came to write, Synge organised his notes by subject, into groups to which he could give titles. 'In doing this,' Edward Stephens notes, 'he did not interfere with the spontaneous quality of his first impressions, but combined recollections so as to make each article an artistic whole, internally balanced like a musical composition.'[9] As a writer Synge was slow. There were days when he managed to put only a few words down on paper but if they were right he was satisifed. Something of a perfectionist, he took his writing through many drafts giving attention to the smallest detail before he was satisfied with the result.[10]

Part One, *In Wicklow,* comprising seven essays, is based on Synge's walks and explorations through the glens and hills of Wicklow. It was here that Synge first developed an interest in the life of countrypeople. In large part these essays are built around the stories he recorded from the people he met along the roads and in the isolated glens. In several of the essays considerable attention is given to tramps and Tinkers, Ireland's indigenous nomads. Synge was one of the few writers of his time to pay attention to the landless people of the road. In these essays we see that Synge idealised the life of the nomad. He believed life in the out-of-doors led to 'good humour and fine bodily health' and that the healthiness of nomadic life led in turn to longevity. The high rate of infant mortality and shorter life span recorded among Tinkers in more recent years suggests the opposite.[11] Synge viewed tramps, somewhat like artists, as repositories of knowledge gathered from the many people they came into contact with during their travels. Although many tramps had taken to the road as a result of some personal failure such as a drinking problem, Synge in *In the Shadow of the Glen* chose to stress the other side. Tramps, he said, are often gifted younger sons driven by their frustrations and creative urges to life on the road. Quite rightly, he considered tramps a genuine value to society for they were a variant to the ordinary way of life. Diversity in lifestyles, he believed, enriched society.

In contrast to the nomads, the peasants of Wicklow are portrayed by Synge as depressed and lonely. They are demoralised by a decline in their population which makes it difficult for the remaining young people to find mates and leaves older people who have lost most of their children to America lonely and isolated. Their 'nervous depression' is compounded, according to Synge, by the damp and rainy climate.

'In a Landlord's Garden' is the only essay in the book dealing with people of Synge's own class. It is based on several summers he spent at Castle Kevin, a boycotted house near Annamoe, Co Wicklow, which like many other Protestant landlord houses of the time was falling into decay and ruin. Though he rebelled against the landlordism of his own family, Synge nevertheless sympathised with the once refined but now declining Protestant ascendancy. 'Everyone is used in Ireland to the tragedy that is bound up with the lives of farmers and fishing people; but in this garden one seemed to feel the tragedy of the landlord class also, and of the innumerable old families that are quickly dwindling away. These owners of the land are not much pitied at the present day, or much deserving of pity; and yet one cannot forget that they are the descendants of what was at one time, in the eighteenth century, a high spirited and highly cultivated aristocracy' (p. 56). Here the image of the ruined landlord class provides a counterpoint to the poverty of the Wicklow peasants.

Part Two, *In West Kerry,* is based on four visits Synge made to the Dingle and Iveragh peninsulas and to the Great Blasket Islands. His first trip took place in the summer of 1903. Afterwards he returned each year until 1907 when his failing health prevented further travel. He first went at the suggestion of his brother, Robert, who had recently returned from a fishing trip to Glenbeigh and thought Synge would find the area and the people interesting. It was at a cottage owned by a man named Philly Harris in Mountain Stage several miles east of Glenbeigh that Synge stayed. Edward Stephens, Synge's nephew, wrote about the visit in his biography. 'When he arrived at Philly Harris's cottage, John was at once aware that he had come among people whose life had the qualities that he had valued in the people of Aran and Wicklow. Their life was not as primitive as that of the islanders, but it had less contact with the outside world than that of any other mainland people he had known. Irish was not generally spoken in the district but they had preserved in English, much traditional lore. . .' [12]

The cottage was an ideal place to stay as it was a gathering place for people in the area and for passers-by. An astute observer with a good ear for dialect, Synge spent many hours jotting down stories, scraps of conversation, figures of speech and even unusual place names from the people who stopped in to visit and pass the time, and from tramps who stayed for the night. He recorded, for example, how a sandy head acquired the name 'Stooks of the Dead Woman' after a boat had come ashore with twelve dead women on board, and how a small hollow came to be named 'Graves of the Sailors' (p. 91). Synge always found great conversation among country people, 'The talk of these people is almost bewildering. . . I often think I have heard all they have to say, and then some one makes a remark that leads to a whole new bundle of folk tales, or stories of wonderful events that have happened in the barony in the last one hundred years' (p. 104). On bicycle he explored the mountain roads around Glenbeigh, and the next summer from his lodging house in Ballyferriter he journeyed on foot to Smerwick, Dunquin, Ventry and Dingle. He spent sixteen days on Great Blasket Island where he stayed in the house of Pádraig Ó Catháin, the headman of the island.

The lore and beliefs Synge presented in his essays are an accurate reflection of what the people actually said. Synge understood the differences between the two main types of story tellers: the *seanchaí* and the *scéalaí*. [13] The first mainly told stories about local occurrences, family sagas and short realistic tales about fairies, ghosts, witches and other imagined supernatural beings. The *scéalaí* who were usually men (the *seanchaí* could be of either sex), told *märchen* or hero tales. These were long stories, difficult to learn, and were usually told in winter when the nights were long and there was little work to be done. They earned the accomplished *scéalaí* high respect in the community. Having examined the folkloristic content of Synge's writings, Seán O'Súilleabháin, one of the deans of Irish folklore, concludes that 'Synge has emerged as a reliable collector of traditional lore. The tales, motifs, verse, folk beliefs and customs are all verifiable as belonging to genuine oral traditions.' [14]

The western end of the Dingle Peninsula where Synge spent much of his time in Kerry was an area in which the majority of the population spoke Irish. Being an Irish-speaker himself he recorded the attitudes of the people about their native tongue. Though Irish had been on the decline for many decades (half the nation's Irish speakers, namely the peasants of the west, had vanished during the Famine) the people were then being encouraged by the newly formed Gaelic League (1893) to use the language and to encourage their children to speak it. Synge records the bewilderment and anger of some countrypeople who as children were punished for speaking Irish, 'When I was a boy they tied a gobban into my mouth for the whole afternoon because I was heard speaking Irish', and were now encouraged to speak nothing but Irish (p. 65). Synge's ability to speak Irish was an advantage to him in developing rapport with country people. Connemara, west Dingle and north-western Mayo were later designated Gaeltachts.

Synge records many of the pastimes of the people, the escapes from routine such as story-telling, horse and mule races, the circus in Dingle and the fair in Killorglin. These pastimes, whatever the specific activity, invariably involved a gathering of people. At Puck Fair, for example, many came to merely walk up and down the streets and gawk at others. In Synge's words, 'A crowd is as exciting as champagne to these lonely people, who live in the long glens among the mountains' (p. 92). As in their work, the country people's pastimes were strongly influenced by the elements. The horse races at Glenbeigh took place between the two tides when the sand was dry. Whether or not Blasket Islanders would get to the races and festivities at Ventry at all depended upon the conditions of the four miles of open sea they had to cross in their skin-covered boats.

Ballad singing and the creation of ballads is treated in several places. Having once aspired to being a musician himself, Synge was particularly interested in the musical talents of the countryfolk. Synge in fact played the piano, flute and violin and had attended the Royal Irish Academy of Music in Dublin for three years where he received a scholarship in harmony and counterpoint. At times he played his fiddle along with the country people. And he greatly enjoyed the dances and wondered at the women in their bare feet moving about on the earthen floors. But of all the pastimes he recorded, drink was the one mentioned most frequently. Drinking, most often poteen but also porter, was a preoccupation of many people. Among the Blasket Islanders, for example, he notes that he never heard the men talk for even half an hour without mentioning drink (p. 82). To drink strong stuff was a sign of manhood. Although drink often led to fighting and was the cause of many accidents at sea, Synge believed it provided an important release.

Part Three, *In Connemara*, consists of twelve essays on the social conditions of one of the most depressed areas of Ireland. These essays were commissioned by the *Manchester Guardian* in 1905. The assignment was to record the living standards of the people and the work of the government's Congested Districts Board which had been set up in 1891 to improve the social and economic conditions of the poorest parts of the country. Jack Yeats, the artist and brother of W. B. Yeats, was hired by the newspaper to make line drawings to illustrate Synge's articles. Together in the summer of 1905 Synge and Yeats travelled for four weeks through

Galway and Mayo. Synge produced three articles per week, each accompanied by one or two of Yeats' drawings. Synge describes his trip in a letter to his friend, Stephen McKenna, '. . . we had a wonderful journey, and as we had a purse to pull on we pushed into out-of-the-way corners in Mayo and Galway that were more strange and marvellous than anything I've dreamed of. Unluckily my commission was to write on the "Distress", so I couldn't do anything like what I would have wished to do as an interpretation of the whole life . . . There are sides of all that western life the groggy-patriot-publican-general shop man who is married to the priest's half sister and is second cousin once-removed of the dispensary doctor, that are horrible and awful. This is the type that is running the present United Irish League anti-grazier campaign while they're swindling the people themselves in a dozen ways and then buying out their holdings and packing off whole families to America . . . All that side of the matter of course I left untouched in my stuff. I sometimes wish to God I hadn't a soul and then I could give myself up to putting those lads on the stage. God, wouldn't they hop! In a way it is all heartrending, in one place the people are starving but wonderfully attractive and charming, and in another place where things are going well one has a rampant double-chinned vulgarity I haven't seen the like of.'[15]

Yeats found Synge a good companion in their explorations. 'Synge was by spirit well equipped for the roads. Though his health was often bad, he had beating under his ribs a brave heart that carried him over rough tracks. He gathered about him very little gear, and cared nothing for comfort except perhaps that of a good turf fire. He was, though young in years, "an old dog for the hard road . . .".'[16] A Dublin publisher named George Roberts asked Synge's permission to reprint the articles in book form. But Synge was not fully satisfied with his own work, and perhaps already considering reworking the articles at a future date, he declined the offer. It was Roberts who published the collected works in 1910.

In assessing the work of the Congested Districts Board, Synge's understanding and empathy for the peasantry, an understanding very uncharacteristic of urban, middle class people of his time, again shows through. Synge did not believe in simple solutions to the problems of the Congested Districts and he particularly opposed the uninformed and sometimes misguided attempts of the Board to bring about reform, particularly when it was imposed on the people. With concern over the Board's recommendations that the thatched roofs of the peasants be replaced with sheets of iron he writes, 'It is far better, wherever possible, to improve the ordinary prosperity of the people till they begin to improve their houses them-selves on their own lines, than to do too much in the way of building houses that have no interest for the people and disfigure the country' (p. 133).

While Synge opposed outsiders meddling in the lives of the country people, he was not shortsighted about the need for change and reform. He recognised that the Board had brought about many improvements, particularly in enlarging farm hold-ings and in constructing roads and bridges which linked the people in these remote areas with the outside world. In his final essay, 'Possible Remedies', he offers some suggestions of his own for raising the standard of living of those in the Congested Districts. In general, his remedies are based on the premise that the peasants know what is best for them. In reference to the Board's attempt to improve livestock in the region, particularly horses and asses, by introducing somewhat haphazardly foreign breeds unsuited to the local environment Synge writes, '. . . it should not be forgotten that the small farmer is not a fool and that he knows perfectly well when he has an animal that is suited to his needs' (p. 150).

Throughout these essays we see evidence that Synge considered life in the countryside with its simplicity and closeness to nature preferable to life in towns and cities. Speaking of west Kerry he writes, 'One wonders in these places why anyone is left in Dublin, or London, or Paris, when it would be better, one would think, to live in a tent or hut with this magnificent sea and sky, and to breathe this wonderful air, which is like wine in one's teeth' (p. 71).

Shy, reserved and unassuming, preferring to remain at the fringes of conversation, John Millington Synge was a private man to the end. He died of Hodgkin's disease in 1909 at the age of thirty-eight, having in a very short career established an international reputation as a dramatist. A scrap of paper found among his papers after his death suggested that he had hoped to re-work the Wicklow and Kerry essays into a book. A year later they were collected along with his articles on Connemara and published posthumously under the title *In Wicklow, West Kerry and Connemara*.

NOTES

1.   Allan Price, *J. M. Synge's Collected Works: Prose,* London: Oxford University Press, 1966.

2.   For a detailed biography of J. M. Synge see David H. Greene and Edward M. Stephens, *J. M. Synge: 1871-1909,* New York: Collier-Macmillan, 1959.

3.   Each summer Synge's mother moved the entire household to Greystones, a fishing village on the Wicklow coast, where they rented lodgings. The family returned to Greystones nearly every year until Synge was 21. It was preferred over the more popular resorts because it was quiet and convenient to relatives at Glanmore Castle, 12 miles to the south. Beginning around 1890 the family took their summers in other locations in Wicklow, notably Castle Kevin near Annamoe.

4.   Table 63, *Census of Ireland, 1901,* London: HMSO.

5.   Joseph Lee, *The Modernisation of Irish Society, 1848-1918,* Dublin: Gill and Macmillan, 1973.

6.   W. E. Vaughan and A. J. Fitzpatrick, *Irish Historical Statistics: Population 1821-1971,* Dublin: Royal Irish Academy, 1978.

7.   J. B. Whittow, *Geology and Scenery of Ireland,* Middlesex: Penguin Books Ltd., 1974.

8.   Ibid., p.183.

9.   Ann Saddlemyer (ed.) 'Synge to MacKenna: The Mature Years', in *Irish Renaissance,* eds. Robin Skelton and David R. Clark, Dublin: Dolmen Press, 1965, pp.72-73.

10. M. H. Crawford, and George Gmelch, 'The Human Biology of the Irish Tinkers: Demography, Ethnohistory and Genetics', *Social Biology,* 21, 1974, pp.321-31.

11. Andrew Carpenter (ed.) *My Uncle John: Edward Stephen's Life of J. M. Synge,* London: Oxford University Press, 1974.

12. Richard Bauman, 'J. M. Synge and Irish Folklore', *Southern Folklore Quarterly,* 18, 1963, pp.267-279.

13. Seán O'Súilleabháin, 'Synge's Uses of Folklore', in *J. M. Synge Centenary Papers,* ed. Maurice Harmon, Dublin: Dolmen Press, 1971.

14. Allan Price, op.cit., p.187.

15. Jack Yeats, 'With Synge in Connemara' in *J. M. Synge: Interviews and Recollections,* ed. Ed Mikhail, London: Macmillan, 1977, pp. 32-34.

16. Ann Saddlemyer, 'Art, Nature and the Prepared Personality', in *Sunshine and the Moon's Delight',* ed. Suheil Bushni, London: Colin Smythe Publishers, 1971, p.108.

The Essays as Literature and Literary Source

Ann Saddlemyer

'Man is naturally a nomad . . . and all wanderers have finer intellectual and physical perceptions than men who are condemned to local habitations,' Synge wrote in his notebook, adding, 'But the vagrant, I think, along with perhaps the sailor, has preserved the dignity of motion with its whole sensation of strange colours in the clouds and of strange passages with voices that whisper in the dark and still stranger inns and lodgings, affections and lonely songs that rest for a whole life time with the perfume of spring evenings or the first autumnal smoulder of the leaves.'[1]

These remarks might well be considered Synge's own ambition and justification. For not only in his travel essays, but woven as a leitmotif through all his plays and much of his poetry is this image of the sensitive wanderer, alert to the entire range of emotions roused by seasons, atmospheres, and elements, responding apparently effortlessly to the most subtle alterations in the complex pattern of time, nature, place, and mood. Synge's traveller, be he playboy (Christy Mahon), mountain herd (Patch Darcy), tinker (Mary Byrne), exile (Deirdre), beggar (Martin and Mary Doul), Tramp (of *The Shadow of the Glen*), or *seanchaí* (of these essays), remains always in tune with his surroundings, conscious of every stop in the vast scale of experience and emotion, deliberately keying his own actions and impressions to the panorama of sky, sea, mountains, birds, beasts and even fellow vagrants. Pitched to an abnormal intensity, he suffers greater joy, experiences keener sensations, reacts with sharper pain, than the Irishman who walks on pavements or stands behind counters. This wanderer is an outcast, Synge insists, by choice and temperament as much as by circumstance: the 'gifted son', either of middle class or peasantry, 'usually a writer or artist with no sense of speculation' (p. 29). He is not to be classed with the drunken flower-women, wily thief, or 'returned American'. He is usually in good humour, and, with the rare painful exception, in good health. Above all, he belongs among abundant nature's variations, not her freaks.

It was among such outcasts that Synge, youngest son of a respectable, professional, evangelical, tightly-knit family, found his spiritual home. Nor despite his career as theatre director, cosmopolitan student, and sometime journalist, did he consider himself merely a week-end vagrant. He had been familiar with every byway of Wicklow since childhood and happily adapted on his journeys westward to the physical discomforts of Aran cottage, Kerry kitchen, and wayside inn. The sympathy inherent in his travel essays comes from the belief that he shares with his companions a common vision of the world about them, which enriches as it isolates and, while remaining mysterious, illuminates. In 'The Oppression of the Hills', for example, he comments on the 'singular way' in which locality shows its influence on the inhabitants of Wicklow, drawing on his own sensitive responses: 'At every season heavy rains fall for often a week at a time, till the thatch drips with water stained to a dull chestnut and the floor in the cottages seems to be going back to the condition of the bogs near it. Then the clouds break, and there is a night of terrific storm from the south-west — all the larches that survive in these places are bowed and twisted towards the point where the sun rises in June — when the winds come down through the narrow glens with the congested whirl and roar of a torrent, breaking at times for sudden moments of silence that keep up the tension of the mind (p. 35).

In such passages from Part One, *In Wicklow,* we find the source for Nora's intensity in *The Shadow of the Glen,* her oppression as the fog lifts momentarily only to overwhelm again in 'the sense of loneliness has no equal' (p. 57), her instant communion with the strange Tramp who has come to terms with this constantly evolving environment:

> TRAMP [*going over to NORA*]   We'll be going now, lady of the house; the rain is falling, but the air is kind, and maybe it'll be a grand morning, by the grace of God.
>
> NORA.   What good is a grand morning when I'm destroyed surely, and I going out to get my death walking the roads?
>
> TRAMP.   You'll not be getting your death with myself, lady of the house, and I knowing all the ways a man can put food in his mouth. . . . We'll be going now, I'm telling you, and the time you'll be feeling the cold, and the frost, and the great rain, and the sun again, and the south wind blowing in the glens, you'll not be sitting up on a wet ditch, the way you're after sitting in this place, making yourself old with looking on each day, and it passing you by. You'll be saying one time, 'It's a grand evening by the grace of God,' and another time, 'It's a wild night, God help us, but it'll pass surely.'

For such travellers, 'the strained feeling of regret one has so often in these places' (p.39) is delicately balanced by the equally solitary splendour afforded by a glimpse of 'a handful of jagged sky filled with extraordinarily brilliant stars' (p.45). And, once again, the bewildering fluctuation of atmosphere is in its turn a constant reminder of the broader spectrums still, of seasons and time itself. 'In these hills the summer passes in a few weeks from a late spring, full of odour and colour, to an autumn that is premature and filled with the desolate splendour of decay', Synge writes in 'The Vagrants of Wicklow'. It is this knowledge of transience that makes old Mary Byrne of *The Tinker's Wedding* wise and Sarah Casey restless:

> SARAH [*angrily*].   Let you not be destroying us with your talk when I've as good a right to a decent marriage as any speckled female does be sleeping in the black hovels above, would choke a mule.
>
> MARY [*soothingly*].   It's as good a right you have surely, Sarah Casey, but what good will it do? Is it putting that ring on your finger will keep you from

getting an aged woman and losing the fine face you have, or be easing your
pains . . .?

Synge's essays in Part Two, *In West Kerry,* reflect the same compassion for a
life daring and basic in its simplicity, sharpened even further by the harsh breath-
taking grandeur of the desolate surroundings. Standing on a cliff on the Great
Blasket Island overlooking the Atlantic, he gasps with delight: 'The whole sight of
wild islands and sea was as clear and cold and brilliant as what one sees in a dream,
and alive with the singularly severe glory that is in the character of this place'
(p. 77). And later, 'At the foot of the cliff a wonderful silvery light was shining
on the sea, which already, before the beginning of autumn, was eager and wintry
and cold. The little group of blue-coated men lying on the grass, and the group of
girls further off, had a singular effect in this solitude of rocks and sea; and in spite
of their high spirits it gave me a sort of grief to feel the utter loneliness and desolation of the place that has given these people their finest qualities' (p. 81). 'The
cold sea and surf, and the feeling of winter in the clouds, and the blackness of the
rocks, and red fern everywhere, were a continual surprise and excitement (p. 107).

In turn, he attempted to capture that singularity (a frequent word in these
essays) in his plays and poems. 'On an Island' accurately describes his little hostess's
activities on the Great Blasket, its rhythm the polka danced the night of his
welcome:

> You've plucked a curlew, drawn a hen,
> Washed the shirts of seven men,
> You've stuffed my pillow, stretched the sheet,
> And filled the pan to wash your feet,
> You've cooped the pullets, wound the clock,
> And rinsed the young men's drinking crock;
> And now we'll dance to jigs and reels,
> Nailed boots chasing girls' naked heels,
> Until your father'll start to snore,
> And Jude, now you're married, will stretch on the floor.

Other poems, such as 'Danny' and 'The Mergency Man' reflect the harshness and
grotesquerie that accompany the wildness and uncompromising severity of Kerry.
But perhaps nowhere more successfully than in *The Playboy of the Western World*
do we find the full range of mood from that 'strange feeling of loneliness' to the
romance the young Blasket girls found in a face 'still raw and bleeding and horrible
to look at'. The combinations of lyricism and earthiness, sudden surprise and sharp
sensibilities developed in the prose essays are skilfully echoed in a rising series of
actions and swooping dialogue steadily widening in range while increasing in
intensity and outrageous candour. The play begins in the stillness of roads and the
desolation of 'the most westerly point of Europe' (p. 66):

SHAWN [*turning towards door again*]. I stood a while outside wondering would I
have a right to pass on or to walk in and see you, Pegeen Mike [*comes to fire*],
and I could hear the cows breathing and sighing in the stillness of the air,
and not a step moving any place from this gate to the bridge.

22

The language and pace grow as Christy Mahon expands from 'a dirty tramp from the highways of the world' into 'a daring fellow is the jewel of the world' with 'such poet's talking, and such bravery of heart'; the play ends with a dazzling burst of imagery, breath-taking reversals, Christy's triumph and Pegeen's sharp awareness of the grief of loss. 'Is it me?' has become 'It is me!' as each character is shaken into fresh insight making the familiar strange and reality mythical.

Synge placed his bitter-sweet comedy in the wilds of Mayo, but the sentiments reflect his travels throughout Ireland and particularly west Kerry, which he visited during the writing of *The Playboy*. The 'singularly brilliant liveliness one meets everywhere in Kerry' (p. 91) is woven also through his rollicking sunlit Wicklow farce, *The Tinker's Wedding*, whose principals confront law and clergy in much the same mood as the old flower-woman challenges the police in the barrack yard and the drunken Blasket Islanders carelessly face the elements on their way home from the fair, or the brawling after the sandhill races. And wild Owen, the grotesque fool of *Deirdre of the Sorrows*, Synge's last play, although emerging from a bog in Wicklow, owes much of his savagery and intensity to Synge's own strong impressions when wandering on the Dingle peninsula: 'The blueness of the sea and the hills from Carrantuohill to the Skelligs, the singular loneliness of the hillside I was on, with a few choughs and gulls in sight only, had a splendour that was almost a grief in the mind' (p. 107).

> OWEN [*sharply*]. Well, go, take your choice. Stay here and rot with Naisi or go to Conchubor in Emain. Conchubor's a wrinkled fool with a swelling belly on him, and eyes falling down from his shining crown; Naisi should be stale and weary. Yet there are many roads, Deirdre, and I tell you I'd sooner be bleaching in a bog-hole than living on without a touch of kindness from your eyes and voice. It's a poor thing to be so lonesome you'd squeeze kisses on a cur dog's nose.

As can be seen from this speech, mad Owen is also perhaps the most poignant spokesman for Synge's tender consciousness of the transitoriness of the life and beauty he felt privileged to observe on his travels. The loss of 'the old knowledge' lamented by his fisherman friend Maurice becomes a major theme also of Part Three, *In Connemara*. 'One's first feeling as one comes back among these people and takes a place, so to speak, in this noisy procession of fishermen, farmers, and women, where nearly everyone is interesting and attractive, is a dread of any reform that would tend to lessen their individuality rather than any very real hope of improving their well-being,' (p. 113) he comments in his introductory article. While reporting with sympathetic, meticulous accuracy the penurious conditions he and Jack Yeats observed during their travels through the Congested Districts, the essays reflect a common warning: change for itself — be it as significant as the introduction of new breeds, new cottages, improved rental system, or as apparently minor as rejection of traditional costume or iron where thatch was once used — must be accompanied by a sympathy for the old familiar methods and traditions. Government officials tend to 'have a traditional misconception of the country people' (p. 137), he notes, advising more care and tactful persuasion in the introduction of new methods (p. 152). Local industries such as fishing, kelp making, pig and potato farming should be subsidised and encouraged before introducing the degradation of relief works, with their thoughtless illogicality which increases shame and melancholy and can only encourage emigration. Describing with delight the kelp makers at work, he remarks pointedly, 'The whole scene, with the fresh smell of the sea and the blueness of the shallow waves, made a curious contrast with the dismal spectacle of the relief workers we had just passed, for here the people seemed as light-hearted as a party of schoolboys (p. 130).

But once a tradition is dead, there is equal fatuousness in attempting to revive it by artificial means. Particularly interesting in the light of his own study of Irish is his conclusion, after quoting various opinions encountered during his travels, that 'this hope of restoring a lost language is a vain one' which can only lead to 'a new kind of hopelessness' and further emigration (p. 154). And, in case there is any doubt of his own political convictions, he ends his series of reports for an English newspaper by expressing his nationalistic and artistic creed: 'One feels that the only real remedy for emigration is the restoration of some national life to the people. It is this conviction that makes most Irish politicians scorn all merely economic or agricultural reforms, for if Home Rule would not of itself make a national life it would do more to make such a life possible than half a million creameries.'

Synge's essays on the Congested Districts are excellent examples of what would now be called 'essay journalism': although written within a comparatively short time (when one considers the months and thousands of typescript pages devoted to painstaking drafts of the plays) they are balanced, considered presentations of the people and conditions in the poorest areas of Ireland. By selecting isolated incidents and striking details, he manages to convey economically and effectively the general situation. Penury is illustrated by its effect: a labourer lights his pipe from a borrowed bit of burning turf, loath to waste a costly match; cottages are built 'on a single sweep of stone with the naked living rock for their floor'; present poverty is set beside memories of the Great Famine through a comparison of the building of the Workhouse with the relief roads; a poor man of Erris speaks of the even poorer conditions of the men who follow the harvest to England. Yet the delight in striking compositions is there too: 'At one corner we came on a group of dark brown asses with panniers, and women standing among them in red dresses, with white or coloured handkerchiefs over their heads; and the whole scene had a strangely foreign, almost Eastern, look, though in its own way it was peculiarly characteristic of Ireland' (p. 143). And always, Synge's keen ear for original language, his joy in the idiosyncracies of such individuals as the ferryman of Dinish Island, the spectacle of bustling towns on market day and profusion of goods in wayside public houses, remind us that the dramatist is alert also. Surely the richness of Christy's prayers, Martin Doul's curses, and the Tramp's invitation have among their sources the old beggarwoman of Spiddal: 'That the blessing of God may be on you, . . . on road and on ridgway, on sea and on land, on flood and on mountain, in all the kingdoms of the world' (p. 114).

In addition to this consistency of vision and mood, as has already been indicated all of Synge's travel essays in turn became a storehouse of imagery, expression, and character later surfacing in his plays. We can trace much of the inspiration for his first completed play, *When the Moon has Set,* to the old Wicklow woman's lament for the passing away of the 'quality' (p. 39), and an overgrown orchard, remnant of 'the tragedy of the landlord class': 'The desolation of this life is often of a peculiarly local kind, and if a playwright chose to go through the Irish country houses he would find material, it is likely, for many gloomy plays' (p. 56). *The Shadow of the Glen* draws upon the fearful oppression of the hills where the prototype for Patch Darcy lived and died; where Nora Burke took comfort from the sight of strangers 'passing up and down over the hill' much as the market-woman did in the sight of Synge himself; and the logic which would prefer a life on the roads to the fine Union below. Throughout the play allusions are made to 'the three shadowy countries that are never forgotten in Wicklow — America (their El Dorado), the Union and the Madhouse' (p. 41); and, like the old woman of Glenmacnass, Nora stores her money in a stocking while her suitor Michael Dara complains of the wilfulness of the mountain ewes. The same essays provide Synge with the story of scheming tinkers which forms the action of *The Tinker's Wedding*, and the aged vagrant's lament for the loss of his long white hair which provided Martin Doul's happy inspiration in the final act of *The Well of the Saints*: 'All his pride and his half-conscious feeling for the dignity of his age seemed to have set themselves on this long hair, which marked him out from the other people of his district; and I have often heard him saying to himself, as he sat beside me under a ditch: "What use is an old man without his hair? A man has only his bloom like the trees; and what use is an old man without his white hair?" ' (p. 31).

> MARTIN DOUL [*bursting with excitement*]. I've this to say, Mary Doul. I'll be letting my beard grow in a short while, a beautiful, long, white, silken, streamy beard, you wouldn't see the like of in the eastern world . . . Ah, a white beard's a grand thing on an old man, a grand thing for making the quality stop and be stretching out their hands with good silver or gold, and a beard's a thing you'll never have, so you may be holding your tongue.

Maurya's well-known conclusion to *Riders to the Sea* may also have its roots in the returned American's excited 'and what more would a man want than that?' (p. 43).

Of all the districts of Ireland, Kerry held the greatest attraction. And so it is not surprising that Synge's most famous play, *The Playboy of the Western World*, although based on a tale told on Aran, draws from the rich storehouse of his west Kerry notebooks. Details such as the use of an iron spoon for a latch (p. 77), the description of racing on the sand (p. 100), topographical references like the Stooks of the Dead Women (p. 91) all find their way into the play. But it was the detailed, 'picturesque and interesting' dialogue Synge admired so much in the cottagers' stories (p. 104) which invaded his work. Blind beggars at Puck Fair share the 'Oriental volubility' of their prayers with Shawn Keogh and Christy Mahon: 'May the Holy Immaculate Mother of Jesus Christ . . . intercede for you in the hour of need. Relieve a poor blind creature, and may Jesus Christ relieve yourselves in the hour of death. May He have mercy, I'm saying, on your brothers and fathers and sisters for evermore (p. 92).

> SHAWN [*at the top of his voice*]. Don't stop me, Michael James. Let me out of the door, I'm saying, for the love of the Almighty God. Let me out [*trying to dodge past him*]. Let me out of it, and may God grant you His indulgence in the hour of need.
> (*The Playboy*, Act I)
> CHRISTY. Aid me to win Pegeen. It's herself only that I'm seeking now. [*Widow Quin gets up and goes to window.*] Aid me for to win her, and I'll

be asking God to stretch a hand to you in the hour of death, and lead you short cuts through the Meadows of Ease, and up the floor of Heaven to the Footstool of the Virgin's Son. *(The Playboy,* Act II)

Again, Synge's host on the Great Blasket instigates not only the following exchange but a hint of characterisation: ' "The young people is no use," he said. "I am not as good a man as my father was, and my son is growing up worse than I am." Then he put up his pipe on the end of the bed-post. "You'll be tired now", he went on, "so it's time we were sleeping; and, I humbly beg your pardon, might I ask your name?" I told him. "Well, good night so," he said, "and may you have a good sleep your first night in this island." ' (p. 78).

> MICHAEL [*going to the door with men*]. And begging your pardon, mister, what name will we call you, for we'd like to know?
> CHRISTY. Christopher Mahon.
> MICHAEL. Well, God bless you, Christy, and a good rest till we meet again when the sun'll be rising to the noon of day. *(The Playboy,* Act I)

Synge was a master story-teller; one of the few activities he emphasises about himself as traveller is his ability to hold his own, whether in telling ghost stories in Irish to the Blasket Islanders (p. 81) or relating the price of fish to eager listeners in a railway carriage (p. 106). We know from scenarios and drafts of incompleted works that, had he lived, even more of the tales he learned on his travels would have found a home in play, essay, or poem.[2] An incident which he included, then regretfully discarded, while writing *The Playboy* concludes his impressionistic essay, 'Glencree': 'I remember lying in the heather one clear Sunday morning in the early autumn when the bracken had just turned. All the people of the district were at Mass in a chapel a few miles away, so the valleys were empty, and there was nothing to be heard but the buzzing of a few late bees and the autumn song of thrushes. The sky was covered with white radiant clouds, with soft outlines, broken in a few places by lines of blue sky of wonderful delicacy and clearness. In a little while I heard a step on a path beneath me, and a tramp came wandering round the bottom of the hill. There was a spring below where I was lying, and when he reached it he looked round to see if anyone was watching him. I was hidden by the ferns, so he knelt down beside the water, where there was a pool among the stones, pulled his shirt over his head, and began washing it in the spring. After a little he seemed satisfied, and began wringing the water out of it; then he put it on, dripping as it was, buttoned his old coat over it, and wandered on towards the village, picking blackberries from the hedge.' (pp. 59-60). In the idyllic, almost prelapsarian setting of the Wicklow morning, the tramp's innocent gesture reflects not only the tenderness Synge felt for his fellow wanderers, but the celebration of a life and simple beauty threatened by time and progress. In his essays, as in his plays, Synge has assured their permanence and his own.

NOTES

1. Quoted by Alan Price in *J. M. Synge Collected Works: Prose,* London: Oxford University Press, 1966, pp.195-96.
2. Additional manuscript material is included in *J. M. Synge Collected Works: Plays, Books One and Two,* ed. Ann Saddlemyer, London: Oxford University Press, 1968. This edition also includes the play *When the Moon Has Set.*

IN WICKLOW

THE VAGRANTS OF WICKLOW

SOME FEATURES OF County Wicklow, such as the position of the principal houses and holiday places on either side of the coach road from Arklow to Bray, have made this district a favourite with the vagrants of Ireland. A few of these people have been on the roads for generations; but fairly often they seem to have merely drifted out from the ordinary people of the villages, and do not differ greatly from the class they come from. Their abundance has often been regretted; yet in one sense it is an interesting sign, for wherever the labourer of a country has preserved his vitality, and begets an occasional temperament of distinction, a certain number of vagrants are to be looked for. In the middle classes the gifted son of a family is always the poorest — usually a writer or artist with no sense for speculation — and in a family of peasants, where the average comfort is just over penury, the gifted son sinks also, and is soon a tramp on the roadside.

In this life, however, there are many privileges. The tramp in Ireland is little troubled by the laws, and lives in out-of-door conditions that keep him in good-humour and fine bodily health. This is so apparent, in Wicklow at least, that these men rarely seek for charity on any plea of ill-health, but ask simply, when they beg: 'Would you help a poor fellow along the road?' or, 'Would you give me the price of a night's lodging, for I'm after walking a great way since the sun rose?'

The healthiness of this life, again, often causes these people to live to a great age, though it is not always easy to test the stories that are told of their longevity. One man, however, who died not long ago, claimed to have reached one hundred and two with a show of likelihood; for several old people remember his first appearance in a certain district as a man of middle age, about the year of the Famine, in 1847 or 1848. This man could hardly be classed with ordinary tramps, for he was married several times in different parts of the world, and reared children of whom he seemed to have forgotten, in his old age, even the names and sex. In his early life he spent thirty years at sea, where he sailed with some one he spoke of after-wards as 'Il mio capitane,' visiting India and Japan, and gaining odd words and intonations that gave colour to his language. When he was too old to wander in the world, he learned all the paths of Wicklow, and till the end of his life he could go the thirty miles from Dublin to the Seven Churches without, as he said, 'putting

4. *Avonmore River*

out his foot on a white road, or seeing any Christian but the hares and moon.' When he was over ninety he married an old woman of eighty-five. Before many days, however, they quarrelled so fiercely that he beat her with his stick, and came out again on the roads. In a few hours he was arrested at her complaint, and sentenced to a month in Kilmainham. He cared nothing for the plank-bed and uncomfortable diet; but he always gathered himself together, and cursed with extraordinary rage, as he told how they had cut off the white hair which had grown down upon his shoulders. All his pride and his half-conscious feeling for the dignity of his age seemed to have set themselves on this long hair, which marked him out from the other people of his district; and I have often heard him saying to himself, as he sat beside me under a ditch: 'What use is an old man without his hair? A man has only his bloom like the trees; and what use is an old man without his white hair?'

Among the country people of the East of Ireland the tramps and tinkers who wander round from the West have a curious reputation for witchery and unnatural powers.

'There's great witchery in that country,' a man said to me once, on the side of a mountain to the east of Aughavanna, in Wicklow. 'There's great witchery in that country, and great knowledge of the fairies. I've had men lodging with me out of the West — men who would be walking the world looking for a bit of money — and every one of them would be talking of the wonders below in Connemara. I remember one time, a while after I was married, there was a tinker down there in the glen, and two women along with him. I brought him into my cottage to do a bit of a job, and my first child was there lying in the bed, and he covered up to his chin with the bedclothes. When the tallest of the women came in, she looked around at him, and then she says —

' "That's a fine boy, God bless him."

' "How do you know it's a boy,' says my woman, "when it's only the head of him you see?"

' "I know rightly," says the tinker, "and it's the first too."

'Then my wife was going to slate me for bringing in people to bewitch her child, and I had to turn the lot of them out to finish the job in the lane.'

I asked him where most of the tinkers came from that are met with in Wicklow.

'They come from every part,' he said. 'They're gallous lads for walking round through the world. One time I seen fifty of them above on the road to Rathdangan, and they all match-making and marrying themselves for the year that was to come. One man would take such a woman, and say he was going such roads and places, stopping at this fair and another fair, till he'd meet them again at such a place, when the spring was coming on. Another, maybe, would swap the woman he had with one from another man, with as much talk as if you'd be selling a cow. It's two hours I was there watching them from the bog underneath, where I was cutting turf, and the like of the crying and the kissing, and the singing and the shouting began when they went off this way and that way, you never heard in your life. Sometimes when a party would be gone a bit down over the hill, a girl would begin crying out and wanting to go back to her ma. Then the man would say: "Black hell to your soul, you've come with me now, and you'll go the whole way." I often seen tinkers before and since, but I never seen such a power of them as were in it that day.'

It need hardly be said that in all tramp life plaintive and tragic elements are common, even on the surface. Some are peculiar to Wicklow. In these hills the summer passes in a few weeks from a late spring, full of odour and colour, to an autumn that is premature and filled with the desolate splendour of decay; and it often happens that, in moments when one is most aware of this ceaseless fading of beauty, some incident of tramp life gives a local human intensity to the shadow of one's own mood.

One evening, on the high ground near the Avonbeg, I met a young tramp just as an extraordinary sunset had begun to fade, and a low white mist was rising from the bogs. He had a sort of table in his hands that he seemed to have made himself out of twisted rushes and a few branches of osier. His clothes were more than usually ragged, and I could see by his face that he was suffering from some terrible disease. When he was quite close, he held out the table.

'Would you give me a few pence for that thing?' he said. 'I'm after working at it all day by the river, and for the love of God give me something now, the way I can get a drink and lodging for the night.'

I felt in my pockets and could find nothing but a shilling piece.

'I wouldn't wish to give you so much,' I said, holding it out to him, 'but it is all I have, and I don't like to give you nothing at all, and the darkness coming on. Keep the table; it's no use to me, and you'll maybe sell it for something in the morning.'

The shilling was more than he expected, and his eyes flamed with joy.

'May the Almighty God preserve you and watch over you and reward you for this night,' he said, 'but you'll take the table; I wouldn't keep it at all, and you after stretching out your hand with a shilling to me, and the darkness coming on.'

He forced it into my hands so eagerly that I could not refuse it, and set off down the road with tottering steps. When he had gone a few yards, I called after him: 'There's your table; take it and God speed you.'

Then I put down his table on the ground, and set off as quickly as I was able. In a moment he came up with me again, holding the table in his hands, and slipped round in front of me so that I could not get away.

'You wouldn't refuse it,' he said, 'and I after working at it all day below by the river.'

He was shaking with excitement and the exertion of overtaking me; so I took his table and let him go his way. A quarter of a mile further on I threw it over the ditch in a desolate place, where no one was likely to find it.

In addition to the more genuine vagrants a number of wandering men and women are to be met with in the northern parts of the county, who walk out for ferns and flowers in bands of from four or five to a dozen. They usually set out in the evening, and sleep in some ditch or shed, coming home the next night with what they have gathered. If their sales are successful, both men and women drink heavily; so that they are always on the edge of starvation, and are miserably dressed, the women sometimes wearing nothing but an old petticoat and shawl — a scantiness of clothing that is sometimes met with also among the road-women of Kerry.

32

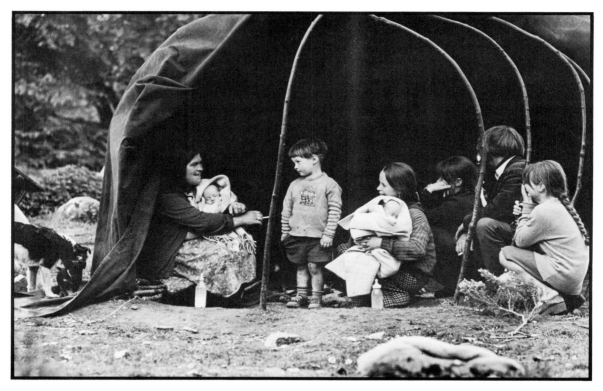

5. Travelling Family

These people are nearly always at war with the police, and are often harshly treated. Once after a holiday, as I was walking home through a village on the border of Wicklow, I came upon several policemen, with a crowd round them, trying to force a drunken flower-woman out of the village. She did not wish to go, and threw herself down, raging and kicking on the ground. They let her lie there for a few moments, and then she propped herself up against the wall, scolding and storming at every one, till she became so outrageous the police renewed their attack. One of them walked up to her and hit her a sharp blow on the jaw with the back of his hand. Then two more of them seized her by the shoulders and forced her along the road for a few yards, till her clothes began to tear off with the violence of the struggle, and they let her go once more.

She sprang up at once when they did so.

'Let this be the barrack's yard, if you wish it,' she cried out, tearing off the rags that still clung about her. 'Let this be the barrack's yard, and come on now, the lot of you.'

Then she rushed at them with extraordinary fury; but the police, to avoid scandal, withdrew into the town, and left her to be quieted by her friends.

Sometimes, it is fair to add, the police are generous and good-humoured. One evening, many years ago, when Whit Monday in Enniskerry was a very different thing from what it is now, I was looking out of a window in that village, watching the police, who had been brought in for the occasion, getting ready to start for Bray. As they were standing out, a young ballad-singer came along from the Dargle, and one of the policemen, who seemed to know him, asked him why a fine stout lad the like of him wasn't earning his bread, instead of straying on the roads.

Immediately the young man drew up on the spot where he was, and began shouting a loud ballad at the top of his voice. The police tried to stop him; but he went on, getting faster and faster, till he ended, swinging his head from side to side, in a furious patter, of which I seem to remember —

> Botheration
> Take the nation,
> Calculation,
> In the stable,
> Cain and Abel,
> Tower of Babel,
> And the Battle of Waterloo.

Then he pulled off his hat, dashed in among the police, and did not leave them till they had all given him the share of money he felt he had earned for his bread.

In all the circumstances of this tramp life there is a certain wildness that gives it romance and a peculiar value for those who look at life in Ireland with an eye that is aware of the arts also. In all the healthy movements of art, variations from the ordinary types of manhood are made interesting for the ordinary man, and in this way only the higher arts are universal. Beside this art, however, founded on the variations which are a condition and effect of all vigorous life, there is another art — sometimes confounded with it — founded on the freak of nature, in itself a

34

mere sign of atavism or disease. This latter art, which is occupied with the antics of the freak, is of interest only to the variation from ordinary minds, and for this reason is never universal. To be quite plain, the tramp in real life, Hamlet and Faust in the arts, are variations; but the maniac in real life, and Des Esseintes and all his ugly crew in the arts, are freaks only.

THE OPPRESSION OF THE HILLS

AMONG THE COTTAGES that are scattered through the hills of County Wicklow I have met with many people who show in a singular way the influence of a particular locality. These people live for the most part beside old roads and pathways where hardly one man passes in the day, and look out all the year on unbroken barriers of heath. At every season heavy rains fall for often a week at a time, till the thatch drips with water stained to a dull chestnut, and the floor in the cottages seems to be going back to the condition of the bogs near it. Then the clouds break, and there is a night of terrific storm from the south-west — all the larches that survive in these places are bowed and twisted towards the point where the sun rises in June — when the winds come down through the narrow glens with the congested whirl and roar of a torrent, breaking at times for sudden moments of silence that keep up the tension of the mind. At such times the people crouch all night over a few sods of turf and the dogs howl in the lanes.

When the sun rises there is a morning of almost supernatural radiance, and even the oldest men and women come out into the air with the joy of children who have recovered from a fever. In the evening it is raining again. This peculiar climate, acting on a population that is already lonely and dwindling, has caused or increased a tendency to nervous depression among the people, and every degree of sadness, from that of the man who is merely mournful to that of the man who has spent half his life in the madhouse, is common among these hills.

Not long ago in a desolate glen in the south of the county I met two policemen driving an ass-cart with a coffin on it, and a little further on I stopped an old man and asked him what had happened.

'This night three weeks,' he said, 'there was a poor fellow below reaping in the glen, and in the evening he had two glasses of whisky with some other lads. Then some excitement took him, and he threw off his clothes and ran away into the hills. There was great rain that night, and I suppose the poor creature lost his way, and was the whole night perishing in the rain and darkness. In the morning they found his naked footmarks on some mud half a mile above the road, and again where you go up by a big stone. Then there was nothing known of him till last night, when they found his body on the mountain, and it near eaten by the crows.'

Then he went on to tell me how different the country had been when he was a young man.

'We had nothing to eat at that time,' he said, 'but milk and stirabout and potatoes, and there was a fine constitution you wouldn't meet this day at all. I

35

6. Near Kilpedder

remember when you'd see forty boys and girls below there on a Sunday evening, playing ball and diverting themselves; but now all this country is gone lonesome and bewildered, and there's no man knows what ails it.'

There are so few girls left in these neighbourhoods that one does not often meet with women that have grown up unmarried. I know one, however, who has lived by herself for fifteen years in a tiny hovel near a cross roads much frequented by tinkers and ordinary tramps. As she has no one belonging to her, she spends a good deal of her time wandering through the country, and I have met her in every direction, often many miles from her own glen. 'I do be so afeard of the tramps,' she said to me one evening. 'I live all alone, and what would I do at all if one of them lads was to come near me? When my poor mother was dying, "Now, Nanny," says she, "don't be living on here when I am dead," says she; "it'd be too lonesome." And now I wouldn't wish to go again' my mother, and she dead — dead or alive I wouldn't go again' my mother — but I'm after doing all I can, and I can't get away by any means.' As I was moving on she heard, or thought she heard, a sound of distant thunder.

'Ah, your honour,' she said, 'do you think it's thunder we'll be having? There's nothing I fear like the thunder. My heart isn't strong — I do feel it — and I have a lightness in my head, and often when I do be excited with the thunder I do be afeard I might die there alone in the cottage and no one know it. But I do hope that the Lord — bless His holy name! — has something in store for me. I've done all I can, and I don't like going again' my mother and she dead. And now good evening, your honour, and safe home.'

Intense nervousness is common also with much younger women. I remember one night hearing some one crying out and screaming in the house where I was staying. I went downstairs and found it was a girl who had been taken in from a village a few miles away to help the servants. That afternoon her two younger sisters had come to see her, and now she had been taken with a panic that they had been drowned going home through the bogs, and she was crying and wailing, and saying she must go to look for them. It was not thought fit for her to leave the house alone so late in the evening, so I went with her. As we passed down a steep hill of heather, where the nightjars were clapping their wings in the moonlight, she told me a long story of the way she had been frightened. When we reached a solitary cottage on the edge of the bog, and as a light was still shining in the window, I knocked at the door and asked if they had seen or heard anything. When they understood our errand three half-dressed generations came out to jeer at us on the doorstep.

'Ah, Maggie,' said the old woman, 'you're a cute one. You're the girl likes a walk in the moonlight. Whist your talk of them big lumps of childer, and look at Martin Edward there, who's not six, and he can go through the bog five times in an hour and not wet his feet.'

My companion was still unconvinced, so we went on. The rushes were shining in the moonlight, and one flake of mist was lying on the river. We looked into one bog-hole, and then into another, where a snipe rose and terrified us. We listened: a cow was chewing heavily in the shadow of a bush, two dogs were barking on the side of a hill, and there was a cart far away upon the road. Our teeth began to chatter with the cold of the bog air and the loneliness of the night. I could see that

7. *Deer Park Glen, Powerscourt*

the actual presence of the bog had shown my companion the absurdity of her fears, and in a little while we went home.

The older people in County Wicklow, as in the rest of Ireland, still show a curious affection for the landed classes wherever they have lived for a generation or two upon their property. I remember an old woman, who told me, with tears streaming on her face, how much more lonely the country had become since the 'quality' had gone away, and gave me a long story of how she had seen her land-lord shutting up his house and leaving his property, and of the way he had died afterwards, when the 'grievance' of it broke his heart. The younger people feel differently, and when I was passing this landlord's house, not long afterwards, I found these lines written in pencil on the door-post:—

> In the days of rack-renting
> And land-grabbing so vile
> A proud, heartless landlord
> Lived here a great while.
> When the League it was started,
> And the land-grabbing cry,
> To the cold North of Ireland
> He had for to fly.

A year later the door-post had fallen to pieces, and the inscription with it.

ON THE ROAD

ONE EVENING after heavy rains I set off to walk to a village at the other side of some hills, part of my way lying along a steep heathery track. The valleys that I passed through were filled with the strange splendour that comes after wet weather in Ireland, and on the tops of the mountains masses of fog were lying in white, even banks. Once or twice I went by a lonely cottage with a smell of earthy turf coming from the chimney, weeds or oats sprouting on the thatch, and a broken cart before the door, with many straggling hens going to roost on the shafts. Near these cottages little bands of half-naked children, filled with the excitement of evening, were running and screaming over the bogs, where the heather was purple already, giving me the strained feeling of regret one has so often in these places when there is rain in the air.

Further on, as I was going up a long hill, an old man with a white, pointed face and heavy beard pulled himself up out of the ditch and joined me. We spoke first about the broken weather and then he began talking in a mournful voice of the famines and misfortunes that have been in Ireland.

'There have been three cruel plagues,' he said, 'out through the country since I was born in the West. First, there was the big wind in 1839, that tore away the grass and green things from the earth. Then there was the blight that came on the

9th of June in the year 1846. Up to then the potatoes were clean and good; but that morning a mist rose up out of the sea, and you could hear a voice talking near a mile off across the stillness of the earth. It was the same the next day, and the day after, and so on for three days or more; and then you could begin to see the tops of the stalks lying over as if the life was gone out of them. And that was the beginning of the great trouble and famine that destroyed Ireland. Then the people went on, I suppose, in their wickedness and their animosity of one against the other; and the Almighty God sent down the third plague, and that was the sickness called the choler. Then all the people left the town of Sligo — it's in Sligo I was reared — and you could walk through the streets at the noon of day and not see a person, and you could knock at one door and another door and find no one to answer you. The people were travelling out north and south and east, with the terror that was on them; and the country people were digging ditches across the roads and driving them back where they could, for they had great dread of the disease.

'It was the law at that time that if there was sickness on any person in the town of Sligo you should notice it to the Governors, or you'd be put up in the gaol. Well, a man's wife took sick, and he went and noticed it. They came down then with bands of men they had, and took her away to the sick-house, and he heard nothing more till he heard she was dead, and was to be buried in the morning. At that time there was such fear and hurry and dread on every person, they were burying people they had no hope of, and they with life within them. My man was uneasy a while thinking on that, and then what did he do, but slip down in the darkness of the night and into the dead-house, where they were after putting his wife. There were beyond twoscore bodies, and he went feeling from one to the other. Then I suppose his wife heard him coming — she wasn't dead at all — and "Is that Michael?" says she. "It is then," says he; "and, oh, my poor woman, have you your last gasps in you still?" "I have, Michael," says she; "and they're after setting me out here with fifty bodies the way they'll put me down into my grave at the dawn of day." "Oh, my poor woman," says he; "have you the strength left in you to hold on my back?" "Oh, Micky," says she, "I have surely." He took her up then on his back, and he carried her out by lanes and tracks till he got to his house. Then he never let on a word about it, and at the end of three days she began to pick up, and in a month's time she came out and began walking about like yourself or me. And there were many people were afeard to speak to her, for they thought she was after coming back from the grave.'

Soon afterwards we passed into a little village, and he turned down a lane and left me. It was not long, however, till another old man that I could see a few paces ahead stopped and waited for me, as is the custom of the place.

'I've been down in Kilpedder buying a scythe-stone,' he began, when I came up to him, 'and indeed Kilpeddar is a dear place, for it's threepence they charged me for it; but I suppose there must be a profit from every trade, and we must all live and let live.'

When we had talked a little more I asked him if he had been often in Dublin.

'I was living in Dublin near ten years,' he said; 'and indeed I don't know what way I lived that length in it, for there is no place which smells like the city of Dublin. One time I went up with my wife into those lanes where they sell old

40

clothing, Hanover Lane and Plunket's Lane, and when my wife — she's dead now, God forgive her! — when my wife smelt the dirty air she put her apron up to her nose, and, "For the love of God," says she, "get me away out of this place." And now may I ask if it's from there you are yourself, for I think by your speaking it wasn't in these parts you were reared?"

I told him I was born in Dublin, but that I had travelled afterwards and been in Paris and Rome, and seen the Pope Leo XIII.

'And will you tell me,' he said, 'is it true that anyone at all can see the Pope?'

I described the festivals in the Vatican, and how I had seen the Pope carried through long halls on a sort of throne. 'Well, now,' he said, 'can you tell me who was the first Pope that sat upon that throne?'

I hesitated for a moment, and he went on:

'I'm only a poor, ignorant man, but I can tell you that myself if you don't know it, with all your travels. Saint Peter was the first Pope, and he was crucified with his head down, and since that time there have been Popes upon the throne of Rome.'

Then he began telling me about himself.

'I was twice a married man,' he said. 'My first wife died at her second child, and then I reared it up till it was as tall as myself — a girl it was — and she went off and got married and left me. After that I was married a second time to an aged woman, and she lived with me ten years, and then she died herself. There is nothing I can make now but tea, and tea is killing me; and I'm living alone, in a little hut beyond, where four baronies, four parishes, and four townlands meet.'

By this time we had reached the village inn, where I was lodging for the night; so I stood him a drink, and he went on to his cottage along a narrow pathway through the bogs.

THE PEOPLE OF THE GLENS

HERE AND THERE in County Wicklow there are a number of little known places — places with curiously melodious names, such as Aughavanna, Glenmalure, Annamoe, or Lough Nahanagan — where the people have retained a peculiar simplicity, and speak a language in some ways more Elizabethan than the English of Connaught, where Irish was used till a much later date. In these glens many women still wear old-fashioned bonnets, with a frill round the face, and the old men, when they are going to the fair, or to Mass, are often seen in curiously-cut frock-coats, tall hats, and breeches buckled at the knee. When they meet a wanderer on foot, these old people are glad to stop and talk to him for hours, telling him stories of the Rebellion, or of the fallen angels that ride across the hills, or alluding to the three shadowy countries that are never forgotten in Wicklow — America (their El Dorado), the Union and the Madhouse.

'I had a power of children,' an old man who was born in Glenmalure, said to me once; 'I had a power of children, and they all went to California, with what I

8. Travelling Woman

could give them, and bought a bit of a field. Then, when they put in the plough, it stuck fast on them. They looked in beneath it, and there was fine gold stretched within the earth. They're rich now and their daughters are riding on fine horses with new saddles on them, and elegant bits in their mouths, yet not a ha'porth did they ever send me, and may the devil ride with them to hell!'

Not long afterwards I met an old man wandering about a hill-side, where there was a fine view of Lough Dan, in extraordinary excitement and good spirits.

'I landed in Liverpool two days ago,' he said, when I had wished him the time of day; 'then I came to the city of Dublin this morning, and took the train to Bray, where you have the blue salt water on your left, and the beautiful valleys, with trees in them, on your right. From that I drove to this place on a jaunting-car to see some brothers and cousins I have living below. They're poor people, Mister, honey, with bits of cabins, and mud floors under them, but they're as happy as if they were in heaven, and what more would a man want than that? In America and Australia, and on the Atlantic Ocean, you have all sorts, good people and bad people, and murderers and thieves, and pickpockets; but in this place there isn't a being isn't as good and decent as yourself or me.'

I saw he was one of the old people one sometimes meets with who emigrated when the people were simpler than they are at present, and who often come back, after a lifetime in the States, as Irish as any old man who has never been twenty miles from the town of Wicklow. I asked him about his life abroad, when we had talked a little longer.

'I've been through perils enough to slay nations,' he said, 'and the people here think I should be rotten with gold, but they're better off the way they are. For five years I was a ship's smith, and never saw dry land, and I in all the danger and peril of the Atlantic Ocean. Then I was a veterinary surgeon, curing side-slip, splay-foot, spavin, splints, glanders, and the various ailments of the horse and ass. The lads in this place think you've nothing to do but to go across the sea and fill a bag with gold; but I tell you it is hard work, and in those countries the workhouses is full, and the prisons is full, and the crazyhouses is full, the same as in the city of Dublin. Over beyond you have fine dwellings, and you have only to put out your hand from the window among roses and vines, and the red wine grape; but there is all sorts in it, and the people is better in this country, among the trees and valleys, and they resting on their floors of mud.'

In Wicklow, as in the rest of Ireland, the union, though it is a home of refuge for the tramps and tinkers, is looked on with supreme horror by the peasants. The madhouse, which they know better, is less dreaded.

One night I had to go down late in the evening from a mountain village to the town of Wicklow, and come back again into the hills. As soon as I came near Rathnew I passed many bands of girls and men making rather ruffianly flirtation on the pathway, and women who surged up to stare at me, as I passed in the middle of the road. The thick line of trees that are near Rathnew makes the way intensely dark, even on clear nights, and when one is riding quickly, the contrast, when one reaches the lights of Wicklow, is singularly abrupt. The town itself after nightfall is gloomy and squalid. Half-drunken men and women stand about, wrangling and disputing in the dull light from the windows, which is only strong enough to show the wretchedness of the figures which pass continually across them. I did my

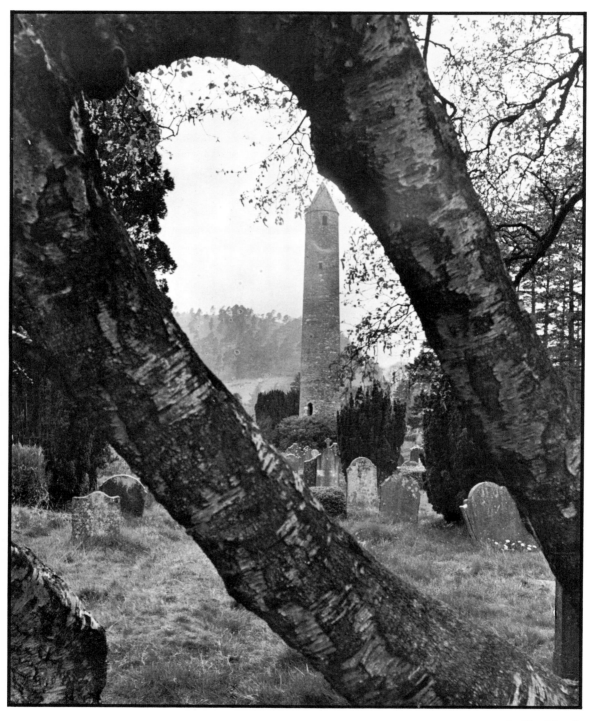

9. *Glendalough*

business quickly and turned back to the hills, passing for the first few miles the same noisy groups and couples on the roadway. After a while I stopped at a lonely public-house to get a drink and rest for a moment before I came to the hills. Six or seven men were talking drearily at one end of the room, and a woman I knew, who had been marketing in Wicklow, was resting nearer the door. When I had been given a glass of beer, I sat down on a barrel near her, and we began to talk.

'Ah, your honour,' she said, 'I hear you're going off in a short time to Dublin, or to France, and maybe we won't be in the place at all when you come back. There's no fences to the bit of farm I have, the way I'm destroyed running. The calves do be straying, and the geese do be straying, and the hens do be straying, and I'm destroyed running after them. We've no man in the place since himself died in the winter, and he ailing these five years, and there's no one to give us a hand drawing the hay or cutting the bit of oats we have above on the hill. My brother Michael has come back to his own place after being seven years in the Richmond Asylum; but what can you ask of him, and he with a long family of his own? And, indeed, it's a wonder he ever came back when it was a fine time he had in the asylum.'

She saw my movement of surprise, and went on:—

'There was a son of my own, as fine a lad as you'd see in the county — though I'm his mother that says it, and you'd never think it to look at me. Well, he was a keeper in a kind of private asylum, I think they call it, and when Michael was taken bad, he went to see him, and didn't he know the keepers that were in charge of him, and they promised to take the best of care of him, and, indeed, he was always a quiet man that would give no trouble. After the first three years he was free in the place, and he walking about like a gentleman, doing any light work he'd find agreeable. Then my son went to see him a second time, and "You'll never see Michael again," says he when he came back, "for he's too well off where he is." And, indeed, it was well for him, but now he's come home.' Then she got up to carry out some groceries she was buying to the ass-cart that was waiting outside.

'It's real sorry I do be when I see you going off,' she said, as she was turning away. 'I don't often speak to you, but it's company to see you passing up and down over the hill, and now may the Almighty God bless and preserve you, and see you safe home.'

A little later I was walking up the long hill which leads to the high ground from Laragh to Sugar Loaf. The solitude was intense. Towards the top of the hill I passed through a narrow gap with high rocks on one side of it and fir trees above them, and a handful of jagged sky filled with extraordinarily brilliant stars. In a few moments I passed out on the brow of the hill that runs behind the Devil's Glen, and smelt the fragrance of the bogs. I mounted again. There was not light enough to show the mountains round me, and the earth seemed to have dwindled away into a mere platform where an astrologer might watch. Among these emotions of the night one cannot wonder that the madhouse is so often named in Wicklow.

Many of the old people of the country, however, when they have no definite sorrow, are not mournful, and are full of curious whims and observations. One old woman who lived near Glen Macanass told me that she had seen her sons had no hope of making a livelihood in the place where they were born, so, in addition to their schooling, she engaged a master to come over the bogs every evening and teach them sums and spelling. One evening she came in behind them, when they were at work and stopped to listen.

'And what do you think my son was after doing?' she said; 'he'd made a sum of how many times a wheel on a cart would turn round between the bridge below and the Post Office in Dublin. Would you believe that? I went out without saying a word, and I got the old stocking, where I kept a bit of money, and I made out what I owed the master. Then I went in again, and "Master," says I, "Mick's learning enough for the likes of him. You can go now and safe home to you." And, God bless you, Avourneen, Mick got a fine job after on the railroad.'

Another day, when she was trying to flatter me, she said: 'Ah, God bless you, Avourneen, you've no pride. Didn't I hear you yesterday, and you talking to my pig below in the field as if it was your brother? And a nice clean pig it is, too, the crathur.' A year or two afterwards I met this old woman again. He husband had died a few months before of the 'Influence,' and she was in pitiable distress, weeping and wailing while she talked to me. 'The poor old man is after dying on me,' she said, 'and he was great company. There's only one son left me now, and we do be killed working. Ah, Avourneen, the poor do have great stratagems to keep in their little cabins at all. And did you ever see the like of the place we live in? Isn't it the poorest, lonesomest, wildest, dreariest bit of a hill a person ever passed a life on?' When she stopped a moment, with the tears streaming on her face, I told a little about the poverty I had seen in Paris.

'God Almighty forgive me, Avourneen,' she went on, when I had finished, 'we don't know anything about it. We have our bit of turf, and our bit of sticks, and our bit to eat, and we have our health. Glory be to His Holy Name, not a one of the childer was ever a day ill, except one boy was hurted off a cart, and he never overed it. It's small right we have to complain at all.'

She died the following winter, and her son went to New York.

The old people who have direct tradition of the Rebellion, and a real interest in it, are growing less numerous daily, but one still meets with them here and there in the more remote districts.

One evening, at the beginning of harvest, as I was walking into a straggling village, far away in the mountains, in the southern half of the county, I overtook an old man walking in the same direction with an empty gallon can. I joined him; and when he had talked for a moment, he turned round and looked at me curiously.

'Begging your pardon, sir,' he said, 'I think you aren't Irish.' I told him he was mistaken.

'Well,' he went on, 'you don't speak the same as we do; so I was thinking maybe you were from another country.'

'I came back from France,' I said, 'two months ago, and maybe there's a trace of the language still upon my tongue.' He stopped and beamed with satisfaction.

'Ah,' he said, 'see that now. I knew there was something about you. I do be talking to all who do pass through this glen, telling them stories of the Rebellion, and the old histories of Ireland, and there's few can puzzle me, though I'm only a poor ignorant man.' He told me some of his adventures, and then he stopped again.

'Look at me now,' he said, 'and tell me what age you think I'd be.'

'You might be seventy,' I said.

'Ah,' he said, with a piteous whine in his voice, 'you wouldn't take me to be

10. *Powerscourt Waterfall*

as old as that? No man ever thought me that age to this day.'

'Maybe you aren't far over sixty,' I said, fearing I had blundered; 'maybe you're sixty-four.' He beamed once more with delight, and hurried along the road.

'Go on, now,' he said, 'I'm eighty-two years, three months and five days. Would you believe that? I was baptized on the fourth of June, eighty-two years ago, and it's the truth I'm telling you.'

'Well, it's a great wonder,' I said, 'to think you're that age, when you're as strong as I am to this day.'

'I am not strong at all,' he went on, more despondingly, 'not strong the way I was. If I had two glasses of whisky I'd dance a hornpipe would dazzle your eyes; but the way I am at this minute you could knock me down with a rush. I have a noise in my head, so that you wouldn't hear the river at the side of it, and I can't sleep at nights. It's that weakens me. I do be lying in the darkness thinking of all that has happened in three-score years to the families of Wicklow — what this son did, and what that son did, and of all that went across the sea, and wishing black hell would seize them that never wrote three words to say were they alive or in good health. That's the profession I have now — to be thinking of all the people, and of the times that's gone. And, begging your pardon, might I ask your name?'

I told him.

'There are two branches of the Synges in the County Wicklow,' he said, and then he went on to tell me fragments of folk-lore connected with my forefathers. How a lady used to ride through Roundwood 'on a curious beast' to visit an uncle of hers in Roundwood Park, and how she married one of the Synges and got her weight in gold — eight stone of gold — as her dowry: stories that referred to events which took place more than a hundred years ago.

When he had finished I told him how much I wondered at his knowledge of the country.

'There's not a family I don't know,' he said, 'from Baltinglass to the sea, and what they've done, and who they've married. You don't know me yet, but if you were a while in this place talking to myself, it's more pleasure and gratitude you'd have from my company than you'd have maybe from many a gentleman you'd meet riding or driving a car.'

By this time we had reached a wayside public-house, where he was evidently going with his can, so, as I did not wish to part with him so soon, I asked him to come in and take something with me. When we went into the little bar-room, which was beautifully clean, I asked him what he would have. He turned to the publican:—

'Have you any good whisky at the present time?' he said.

'Not now; nor at any time,' said the publican; 'we only keep bad; but isn't it all the same for the likes of you that wouldn't know the difference?'

After prolonged barging he got a glass of whisky, took off his hat before he tasted it, to say a prayer for my future, and then sat down with it on a bench in the corner.

I was served in turn, and we began to talk about horses and racing, as there had been races in Arklow a day or two before. I alluded to some races I had seen in France, and immediately the publican's wife, a young woman who had just come in, spoke of a visit she had made to the Grand Prix a few years before.

'Then you have been in France?' I asked her.

'For eleven years,' she replied.

'Alors vous parlez Français, Madame?'

'Mais oui, Monsieur,' she answered with pure intonation.

We had a little talk in French, and then the old man got his can filled with porter — the evening drink for a party of reapers who were working on the hill — bought a pennyworth of sweets, and went back down the road.

'That's the greatest old rogue in the village,' said the publican, as soon as he was out of hearing; 'he's always making up to all who pass through the place, and trying what he can get out of them. The other day a party told me to give him a bottle of XXX porter he was after asking for. I just gave him the dregs of an old barrel we had finished, and there he was, sucking in his lips, and saying it was the finest drink ever he tasted, and that it was rising to his head already, though he'd hardly a drop of it swallowed. Faith in the end I had to laugh to hear the talk he was making.'

A little later I wished them good evening and started again on my walk, as I had two mountains to cross.

AT A WICKLOW FAIR
THE PLACE AND THE PEOPLE

A YEAR OR TWO ago I wished to visit a fair in County Wicklow, and as the buying and selling in these fairs are got through very early in the morning I started soon after dawn to walk the ten or twelve miles that led to Aughrim, where the fair was to be held. When I came out into the air the cold was intense, though it was a morning of August, and the dew was so heavy that bushes and meadows of mountain grass seemed to have lost their greenness in silvery grey. In the glens I went through white mists were twisting and feathering themselves into extra-ordinary shapes, and showing blue hills behind them that looked singularly desolate and far away. At every turn I came on multitudes of rabbits feeding on the road-side, or on even shyer creatures — corncrakes, squirrels and snipe — close to villages where no one was awake.

Then the sun rose, and I could see lines of smoke beginning to go up from farmhouses under the hills, and sometimes a sleepy, half-dressed girl looked out of the door of a cottage when my feet echoed on the road. About six miles from Aughrim I began to fall in with droves of bullocks and sheep, in charge of two or three dogs and a herd, or with whole families of mountain people, driving nothing but a single donkey or kid. These people seemed to feel already the animation of the fair, and were talking eagerly and gaily among themselves. I did not hurry, and it was about nine o'clock when I made my way into the village, which was now thronged with cattle and sheep. On every side the usual half-humorous bargaining could be heard above the noise of the pigs and donkeys and lambs. One man would say: 'Are you going to not divide a shilling with me? Are you going to not do it?

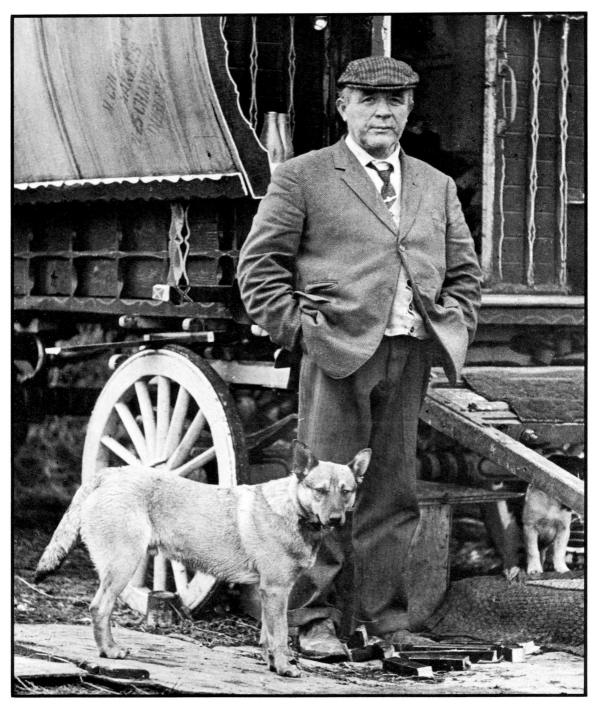

11. A Travelling Man

You're the biggest schemer ever walked down into Aughrim.'

A little further on a man said to a seller: 'You're asking too much for them lambs.' The seller answered: 'If I didn't ask it how would I ever get it? The lambs is good lambs, and if you buy them now you'll get home nice and easy in time to have your dinner in comfort, and if you don't buy them you'll be here the whole day sweating in the heat and dust, and maybe not please yourself in the end of all.'

Then they began looking at the lambs again, talking of the cleanness of their skin and the quality of the wool, and making many extravagant remarks in their praise or against them. As I turned away I heard the loud clap of one hand into another, which always marks the conclusion of a bargain.

A little further on I found a farmer I knew standing before a public-house, looking radiant with delight. 'It's a fine fair, Mister,' he said, 'and I'm after selling the lambs I had here a month ago and no one would look at them. Then I took them to Rathdrum and Wicklow, getting up at three in the morning, and driving them in the creel, and it all for nothing. But I'm shut of them now, and it's not too bad a price I've got either. I'm after driving the lambs outside the customs (the boundary where the fair tolls are paid), and I'm waiting now for my money.' While we were talking, a cry of warning was raised: 'Mind yourselves below; there's a drift of sheep coming down the road.' Then a couple of men and dogs appeared, trying to drive a score of sheep that some one had purchased, out of the village, between the countless flocks that were standing already on either side of the way. This task is peculiarly difficult. Boys and men collect round the flock that is to be driven out, and try to force the animals down the narrow passage that is left in the middle of the road. It hardly ever happens, however, that they get through without carrying off a few of some one else's sheep, or losing some of their own, which have to be restored, or looked for afterwards.

The flock was driven by as well as could be managed, and a moment later an old man came up to us, and asked if we had seen a ewe passing from the west. 'A sheep is after passing,' said the farmer I was talking to, 'but it was not one of yours, for it was too wilful; it was a mountain sheep.' Sometimes animals are astray in this way for a considerable time — it is not unusual to meet a man the day after a fair wandering through the country, asking after a lost heifer, or ewe — but they are always well marked and are found in the end.

When I reached the green above the village I found the curious throng one always meets in these fairs, made up of wild mountain squatters, gentlemen farmers, jobbers and herds. At one corner of the green there was the usual camp of tinkers, where a swarm of children had been left to play among the carts while the men and women wandered through the fair selling cans or donkeys. Many odd types of tramps and beggars had come together also, and were loitering about in the hope of getting some chance job, or of finding some one who would stand them a drink. Once or twice a stir was made by some unruly ram or bull, but in these smaller fairs there seldom is much real excitement till the evening, when the bad whisky that is too freely drunk begins to be felt.

When I had spoken to one or two men that I wished to see, I sat down near a bridge at the end of the green, between a tinker who was mending a can and a herd who was minding some sheep that had not been sold. The herd spoke to me with some pride of his skill in dipping sheep to keep them from the fly, and other

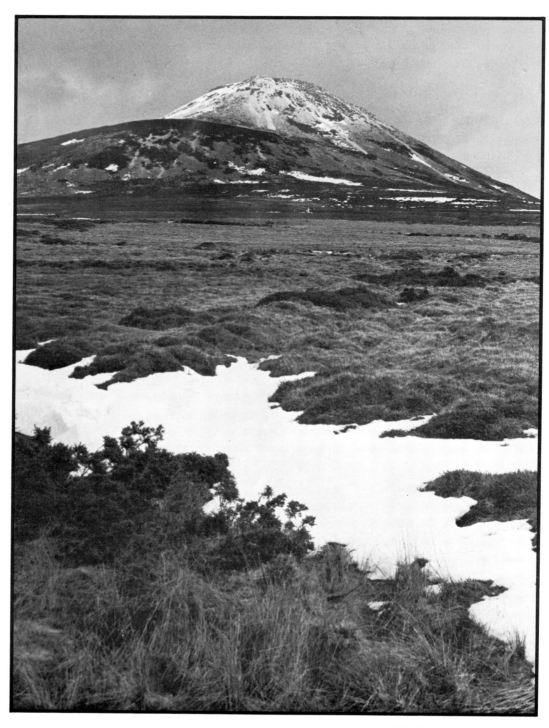

12. Great Sugarloaf Mountain

matters connected with his work. 'Let you not be talking,' said the tinker, when he paused for a moment. 'You've been after sheep since you were that height (holding his hand a little over the ground), and yet you're nowhere in the world beside the herds that do be reared beyond on the mountains. Those men are a wonder, for I'm told they can tell a lamb from their own ewes before it is marked, and that when they have five hundred sheep on the hills — five hundred is a big number — they don't need to count them or reckon them at all, but they just walk here and there where they are, and if one is gone away they'll miss it from the rest.'

Then a woman came up and spoke to the tinker, and they went down the road together into the village. 'That man is a great villain,' said the herd, when he was out of hearing. 'One time he and his woman went up to a priest in the hills and asked him would he wed them for half a sovereign, I think it was. The priest said it was a poor price, but he'd wed them surely if they'd make him a tin can along with it. "I will, faith," said the tinker, "and I'll come back when it's done." They went off then, and in three weeks they came back, and they asked the priest a second time would he wed them. "Have you the tin can?" said the priest. "We have not," said the tinker; "we had it made at the fall of night, but the ass gave it a kick this morning the way it isn't fit for you at all." "Go on now," says the priest. "It's a pair of rogues and schemers you are, and I won't wed you at all." They went off then, and they were never married to this day.'

As I went up again through the village a great sale of old clothing was going on from booths at each side of the road, and further on boots were set out for sale on boards laid across the tops of barrels, a very usual counter. In another place old women were selling quantities of damaged fruit, kippered herrings, and an extraordinary collection of old ropes and iron. In front of a public-house a ballad-singer was singing a song in the middle of a crowd of people. As far as I could hear it, the words ran like this: —

As we came down from Wicklow
With our bundle of switches;
As we came down from Wicklow,
Oh! what did we see?
As we came to the city
We saw maidens pretty,
And we called out to ask them to buy our heath-broom.
Heath-broom, freestone, black turf, gather them up.

Oh! gradh machree, Mavourneen
Won't you buy our heath-broom?

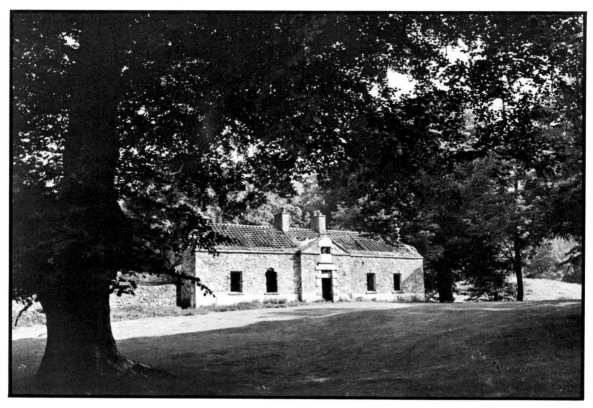

13. Servants Quarters, Powerscourt

When the season is over
Won't we be in clover,
With the gold in our pockets
We got from heath-broom.
It's home we will toddle,
And we'll get a naggin,
And we'll drink to the maidens that bought our heath-broom.
Heath-broom, freestone, black turf, gather them up.

Oh! gradh machree, Mavourneen,
Won't you buy our heath-broom?

Before he had finished a tinker arrived, too drunk to stand or walk, but leading a tall horse with his left hand, and inviting anyone who would deny that he was the best horseman in Wicklow to fight with him on the spot. Soon afterwards I started on my way home, driving most of the way with a farmer from the same neighbourhood.

A LANDLORD'S GARDEN
IN COUNTY WICKLOW

A STONE'S THROW from an old house where I spent several summers in County Wicklow, there was a garden that had been left to itself for fifteen or twenty years. Just inside the gate, as one entered, two paths led up through a couple of strawberry beds, half choked with leaves, where a few white and narrow strawberries were still hidden away. Further on was nearly half an acre of tall raspberry canes and thistles five feet high, growing together in a dense mass, where one could still pick raspberries enough to last a household for the season. Then, in a waste of hemlock, there were some half-dozen apple trees covered with lichen and moss, and against the northern walls a few dying plum trees hanging from their nails. Beyond them there was a dead pear tree, and just inside the gate, as one came back to it, a large fuchsia filled with empty nests. A few lines of box here and there showed where the flower-beds had been laid out, and when anyone who had the knowledge looked carefully among them many remnants could be found of beautiful and rare plants.

All round this garden there was a wall seven or eight feet high, in which one could see three or four tracks with well-worn holes, like the paths down a cliff in Kerry, where boys and tramps came over to steal and take away any apples or other fruits that were in season. Above the wall on the three windy sides there were rows of finely-grown lime trees, the place of meeting in the summer for ten thousand bees. Under the east wall there was the roof of a green house, where one could sit, when it was wet or dry, and watch the birds and butterflies, many of which were not common. The seasons were always late in this place — it was high above the sea — and redpoles often used to nest not far off late in the summer; siskins did the same once or twice, and greenfinches, till the beginning of August, used to cackle endlessly in the lime trees.

Everyone is used in Ireland to the tragedy that is bound up with the lives of farmers and fishing people; but in this garden one seemed to feel the tragedy of the landlord class also, and of the innumerable old families that are quickly dwindling away. These owners of the land are not much pitied at the present day, or much deserving of pity; and yet one cannot quite forget that they are the descendants of what was at one time, in the eighteenth century, a high-spirited and highly-cultivated aristocracy. The broken greenhouses and mouse-eaten libraries, that were designed and collected by men who voted with Grattan, are perhaps as mournful in the end as the four mud walls that are so often left in Wicklow as the only remnants of a farmhouse. The desolation of this life is often of a peculiarly local kind, and if a playwright chose to go through the Irish country houses he would find material, it is likely, for many gloomy plays that would turn on the dying away of these old families, and on the lives of the one or two delicate girls that are left so often to represent a dozen hearty men who were alive a generation or two ago. Many of the descendants of these people have, of course, drifted into professional life in Dublin, or have gone abroad; yet, wherever they are, they do not equal their forefathers, and where men used to collect fine editions of *Don Quixote* and Moliere, in Spanish and French, and luxuriantly bound copies of Juvenal and Persius and Cicero, nothing is read now but Longfellow and Hall Caine and Miss Corelli. Where good and roomy houses were built a hundred years ago, poor and tawdry houses are built now; and bad bookbinding, bad pictures, and bad decorations are thought well of, where rich bindings, beautiful miniatures and finely-carved chimney-pieces were once prized by the old Irish landlords.

To return to our garden. One year the apple crop was unusually plentiful, and every Sunday inroads were made upon it by some unknown persons. At last I decided to lie in wait at the dangerous hour — about twelve o'clock — when the boys of the neighbourhood were on their way home from Mass, and we were supposed to be busy with our devotions three miles away. A little before eleven I slipped out, accordingly, with a book, locked the door behind me, put the key in my pocket and lay down under a bush. When I had been reading for some time, and had quite forgotten the thieves, I looked up at some little stir and saw a young man, in his Sunday clothes, walking up the path towards me. He stopped when he saw me, and for a moment we gazed at each other with astonishment. At last, to make a move, I said it was a fine day. 'It is indeed, sir,' he answered with a smile, and then he turned round and ran for his life. I realized that he was a thief, and jumped up and ran after him, seeing, as I did so, a flock of small boys swarming up the walls of the garden. Meanwhile the young man ran round and round through the raspberry canes, over the strawberry beds and in and out among the apple trees. He knew that if he tried to get over the wall I should catch him, and that there was no other way out, as I had locked the gate. It was heavy running, and we both began to get weary. Then I caught my foot in a briar and fell. Immediately the young man rushed to the wall and began scrambling up it, but just as he was drawing his leg over the top I caught him by the heel. For a moment he struggled and kicked, then by sheer weight I brought him down at my feet, and an armful of masonry along with him. I caught him by the neck and tried to ask his name, but found we were too breathless to speak.

For I do not know how long we sat glaring at each other, and gasping painfully. Then by degrees I began to upbraid him in a whisper for coming over a person's wall to steal his apples, when he was such a fine well-dressed, grown-up young man. I could see that he was in mortal dread that I might have him up in the police courts, which I had no intention of doing, and when I finally asked him his name and address he invented a long story of how he lived six miles away, and had come over to this neighbourhood for Mass and to see a friend, and then how he had got a drought upon him, and thought an apple would put him in spirits for his walk home. Then he swore he would never come over the wall again if I would let him off, and that he would pray God to have mercy on me when my last hour was come. I felt sure his whole story was a tissue of lies, and I did not want him to have the crow of having taken me in. 'There is a woman belonging to the place,' I said, 'inside in the house helping the girl to cook the dinner. Walk in now with me, and we'll see if you're such a stranger as you'd have me think.' He looked infinitely troubled, but I took him by the neck and wrist and we set off for the gate. When we had gone a pace or two he stopped. 'I beg your pardon,' he said, 'my cap's after falling down on the over side of the wall. May I cross over and get it?' That was too much for me. 'Well, go on,' I said, 'and if ever I catch you again woe betide you.' I let him go then, and he rushed madly over the wall and disappeared. A few days later I discovered, not at all to my surprise, that he lived half a mile away, and was intimately related to a small boy who came to the house every morning to run messages and clean the boots. Yet it must not be thought that this young man was dishonest; I would have been quite ready the next day to trust him with a ten-pound note.

GLENCREE

THIS MORNING the air is clear, and there is a trace of summer again. I am sitting in a nook beside the stream from the Upper Lake, close down among the heather and bracken and rushes. I have seen the people going up to Mass in the Reformatory and the valley seems empty of life.

I have gone on, mile after mile, of the road to Sally Gap, between brown dikes and chasms in the turf, with broken foot-bridges across them, or between sheets of sickly moss and bog-cotton that is unable to thrive. The road is caked with moss that breaks like pie-crust under my feet, and in corners where there is shelter there are sheep loitering, or a few straggling grouse . . . The fog has come down in places; I am meeting multitudes of hares that run round me at a little distance — looking enormous in the mists — or sit up on their ends against the sky line to watch me going by. When I sit down for a moment the sense of loneliness has no equal. I

14. Glencree

15. Glencree

can hear nothing but the slow running of water and the grouse crowing and chuckling underneath the band of cloud. Then the fog lifts and shows the white empty roads winding everywhere, with the added sense of desolation one gets passing an empty house on the side of a road.

When I turn back again the air has got stuffy and heavy and calm, with a cloud still down upon the glen; there is a dead heat in the air that is not natural so high up, and the silence is so great three or four wrens that are singing near the lake seem to fill the valley with sound. In most places I can see the straight ending of the cloud, but above the lake grey fingers are coming up and down like a hand that is clasping and opening again. One longs for rain or wind or thunder. The very ewes and lambs have stopped bleating, and are slinking round among the stacks of turf.

I have come out again on the mountain road the third day of the fog. At first it was misty only, and then a cloud crept up the water gullies from the valley of the Liffey, and in a moment I am cut off in a white silent cloud. The little turfy ridges on each side of the road have the look of glens to me, and every block of stone has the size of a house. The cobwebs on the furze are like a silvery net, and the silence is so great and queer, even weazels run squealing past me on the side of the road. . . . An east wind is rising. Once in every minute I see the little mounds in their natural shapes that have been mountains for a week. I see wet cottages on the other side of the glen that I had forgotten. Then, as I walk on, I see out over a cloud to the tops of real mountains standing up into the sky.

There is a dense white fog around the cottage, and we seem to be shut away from any habitation. All round behind the hills there is a moan and rumble of thunder coming nearer, at times with a fierce and sudden crash. The bracken has a nearly painful green in the strangeness of the light. Enormous sheep are passing in and out of the sky line.

There is a strange depression about the cottage to-night. The woman of the house is taken ill and has got into bed beside her mother-in-law, who is over ninety and is wandering in her mind. The man of the house has gone away ten miles for medicine, and I am left with the two children, who are playing silently about the door.

The larches in the haggard are dripping heavily with damp, and the hens and geese, bewildered with the noise and gloom, are cackling with uneasy dread. All one's senses are disturbed. As I walk backwards and forwards, a few yards above and below the door, the little stream I do not see seems to roar out of the cloud.

Every leaf and twig is heavy with drops, and a dog that has passed with a sad-eyed herd looks wet and draggled and afraid.

I remember lying in the heather one clear Sunday morning in the early autumn when the bracken had just turned. All the people of the district were at Mass in a chapel a few miles away, so the valleys were empty, and there was nothing to be heard but the buzzing of a few late bees and the autumn song of thrushes. The sky was covered with white radiant clouds, with soft outlines, broken in a few

16. Enniskerry

places by lines of blue sky of wonderful delicacy and clearness. In a little while I heard a step on a path beneath me, and a tramp came wandering round the bottom of the hill. There was a spring below where I was lying, and when he reached it he looked round to see if anyone was watching him. I was hidden by the ferns, so he knelt down beside the water, where there was a pool among the stones, pulled his shirt over his head, and began washing it in the spring. After a little he seemed satisfied, and began wringing the water out of it; then he put it on, dripping as it was, buttoned his old coat over it, and wandered on towards the village, picking blackberries from the hedge.

IN WEST KERRY

AT TRALEE STATION — I was on my way to a village many miles beyond Dingle — I found a boy who carried my bag some way along the road to an open yard where the light railway starts for the west. There was a confused mass of peasants struggling on the platform, with all sort of baggage, which the people lifted into the train for themselves as well as they were able. The seats ran up either side of the cars, and the space between them was soon filled with sacks of flour, cases of porter, chairs rolled in straw, and other household goods. A drunken young man got in just before we started, and sang songs for a few coppers, telling us that he had spent all his money, and had nothing left to pay for his ticket. Then, when the carriage was closely packed, we moved slowly out of the station. At my side there was an old man who explained the Irish names of the places that we came to, and pointed out the Seven Pigs, a group of islands in the bay; Kerry Head, further off; and many distant mountains. Beyond him a dozen big women in shawls were crowded together; and just opposite me there was a young woman wearing a wedding ring, who was one of the peculiarly refined women of Kerry, with supreme charm in every movement and expression. The big woman talked to her about some elderly man who had been sick — her husband, it was likely — and some young man who had gone away to England, and was breaking his heart with loneliness.

'Ah, poor fellow!' she said; 'I suppose he will get used to it like another; and wouldn't he be worse off if he was beyond the seas in Saint Louis, or the towns of America?'

This woman seemed to unite the healthiness of the country people with the greatest sensitiveness, and whenever there was any little stir or joke in the carriage, her face and neck flushed with pleasure and amusement. As we went on there were superb sights — first on the north, towards Loop Head, and then when we reached the top of the ridge, to the south also, to Drung Hill, Macgillicuddy's Reeks, and other mountains of South Kerry. A little further on, nearly all the people got out at a small station; and the young woman I had admired gathered up most of the household goods and got down also, lifting heavy boxes with the power of a man. Then two returned American girls got in, fine, stout-looking women, with distress in their expression, and we started again. Dingle Bay could now be seen through

17. *Roving Swan, Dingle*

narrow valleys on our left, and had extraordinary beauty in the evening light. In the carriage next to ours a number of herds and jobbers were travelling, and for the last hour they kept up a furious altercation that seemed always on the verge of breaking out into a dangerous quarrel, but no blows were given.

At the end of the line an old blue side-car was waiting to take me to the village where I was going. I was some time fastening on my goods, with the raggedy boy who was to drive me; and then we set off, passing through the usual streets of a Kerry town, with public-houses at the corners, till we left the town by a narrow quay with a few sailing boats and a small steamer with coal. Then we went over a bridge near a large water-mill, where a number of girls were standing about, with black shawls over their heads, and turned sharp to the right, against the face of the mountains. At first we went up hill for several miles, and got on slowly, though the boy jumped down once or twice and gathered a handful of switches to beat the tall mare he was driving. Just as the twilight was beginning to deepen we reached the top of the ridge and came out through a gap into sight of Smerwick Harbour, a wild bay with magnificent headlands beyond it, and a long stretch of the Atlantic. We drove on towards the west, sometimes very quickly, where the slope was gradual, and then slowly again when the road seemed to fall away under us, like the wall of a house. As the night fell the sea became like a piece of white silver on our right; and the mountains got black on our left, and heavy night smells began to come up out of the bogs. Once or twice I noticed a blue cloud over the edge of the road, and then I saw that we were nearly against the gables of a little village, where the houses were so closely packed together there was no light from any of them. It was now quite dark, and the boy got cautious in his driving, pulling the car almost into the ditch once or twice to avoid an enormous cavity where the middle of the road had settled down into the bogs. At last we came to another river and a public-house and went up a hill, from which we could see the outline of a chapel; then the boy turned to me: 'Is it ten o'clock yet?' he said; 'for we're mostly now in the village.'

This morning, a Sunday, rain was threatening; but I went out west after my breakfast under Croagh Martin, in the direction of the Atlantic. At one of the first villages I came to I had a long talk with a man who was sitting on the ditch waiting till it was time for Mass. Before long we began talking about the Irish language.

'A few years ago,' he said, 'they were all for stopping it off; and when I was a boy they tied a gobban into my mouth for the whole afternoon because I was heard speaking Irish. Wasn't that great cruelty? And now when I hear the same busy-bodies coming around and telling us for the love of God to speak nothing but Irish, I've a good mind to tell them to go to hell. There was a priest out here a while since who was telling us to stay always where we are, and to speak nothing but Irish; but, I suppose, although the priests are learned men, and great scholars, they don't understand the life of the people the same as another man would. In this place the land is poor — you can see that for yourself — and the people have little else to live on; so that when there is a long family, one son will stay at home and keep on the farm, and the others will go away because they must go. Then when they once pass out of the Dingle station in Tralee they won't hear a word of Irish, or meet anyone who'd understand it; so what good, I ask you, is a man who hasn't got the English, and plenty of it?'

After I left him I went on towards Dunquin, and lay for a long time on the side of a magnificently wild road under Croagh Martin, where I could see the Blasket Islands and the end of Dunmore Head, the most westerly point of Europe. It was a grey day with a curious silence on the sea and sky and no sign of life anywhere, except the sail of one curagh — or niavogue, as they are called here — that was sailing in from the islands. Now and then a cart passed me filled with old people and children, who saluted me in Irish; then I turned back myself. I got on a long road running through a bog, with a smooth mountain on one side and the sea on the other, and Brandon in front of me, partly covered with clouds. As far as I could see there were little groups of people on their way to the chapel in Bally-ferriter, the men in homespun and the women wearing blue cloaks, or, more often, black shawls twisted over their heads. This procession along the olive bogs, between the mountains and the sea, on this grey day of autumn, seemed to wring me with the pang of emotion one meets everywhere in Ireland — an emotion that is partly local and patriotic, and partly a share of the desolation that is mixed everywhere with the supreme beauty of the world.

In the evening, when I was walking about the village, I fell in with a man who could read Gaelic, and was full of enthusiasm for the old language and of contempt for English.

'I can tell you,' he said, 'that the English I have is no more good to me than the cover of that pipe. Buyers come here from Dingle and Cork and Clare, and they have good Irish, and so has everyone we meet with, for there is no one can do business in this place who hasn't the language on his tongue.'

Then I asked him about the young men who go away to America.

'Many go away,' he said, 'who could stay if they wished to, for it is a fine place for fishing, and a man will get more money and better health for himself, and rear a better family, in this place than in many another. It's a good place to be in, and now, with the help of God, the little children will all learn to read and write in Irish, and that is a great thing, for how can people do any good, or make a song even, if they cannot write? You will be often three weeks making a song, and there will be times when you will think of good things to put into it that could never be beaten in the whole world; but if you cannot write them down you will forget them, maybe, by the next day, and then what good will be your song?'

After a while we went upstairs to a large room in the inn, where a number of young men and girls were dancing jigs and reels. These young people, although they are as Irish-speaking as the people of Connemara, are pushing forward in their ways of living and dress; so that this group of dancers could hardly have been known, by their appearance, from any Sunday party in Limerick or Cork. After a long four-hand reel, my friend, who was dressed in homespun, danced a jig to the whistling of a young man with great energy and spirit. Then he sat down beside me in the corner, and we talked about spring trawling and the price of nets. I told him about the ways of Aran and Connemara; and then he told me about the French trawlers who come to this neighbourhood in April and May.

'The Frenchmen from Fécamp,' he said, 'are Catholics and decent people; but those who come from Boulogne have no religion, and are little better than a wild beast would lep on you out of a wood. One night there was a drift of them

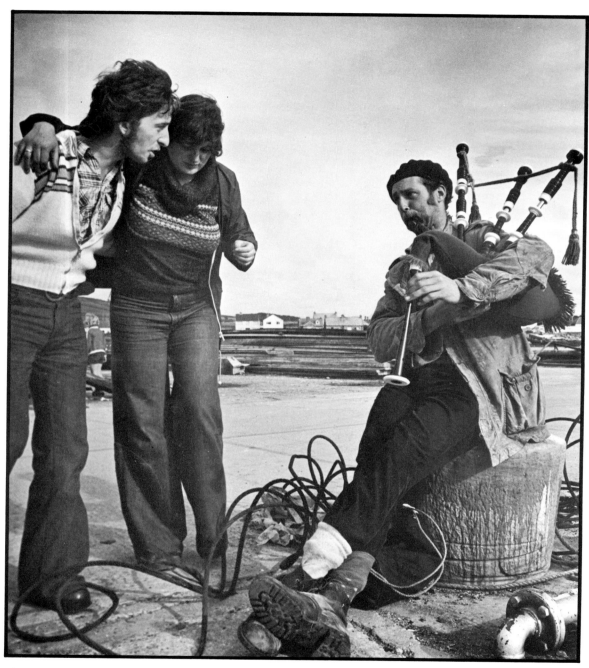

18. Dingle Piper

below in the public-house, where there is a counter, as you've maybe seen, with a tin top on it. Well, they were talking together, and they had some little difference among themselves, and from that they went on raising their voices, till one of them out with his knife and drove it down through the tin into the wood! Wasn't that a dangerous fellow?'

Then he told me about their tobacco.

'The French do have two kinds of tobacco; one of them is called hay-tobacco, and if you give them a few eggs, or maybe nine little cabbage plants, they'll give you as much of it as would fill your hat. Then we get a pound of our own tobacco and mix the two of them together, and put them away in a pig's bladder — it's that way we keep our tobacco — and we have enough with that lot for the whole winter.'

This evening a circus was advertised in Dingle, for one night only; so I made my way there towards the end of the afternoon, although the weather was windy and threatening. I reached the town an hour too soon, so I spent some time watching the wild-looking fishermen and fishwomen who stand about the quays. Then I wandered up and saw the evening train coming in with the usual number of gaily-dressed young women and half-drunken jobbers and merchants; and at last, about eight o'clock, I went to the circus field, just above the town, in a heavy splash of rain. The tent was set up in the middle of the field, and a little to the side of it a large crowd was struggling for tickets at one of the wheeled houses in which the acrobats live. I went round the tent in the hope of getting in by some easier means, and found a door in the canvas, where a man was calling out: 'Tickets, or money, this way,' and I passed in through a long winding passage. It was some time after the hour named for the show, but although the tent was almost filled there was no sign of the performers; so I stood back in a corner and watched the crowd coming in wet and dripping from the rain, which had turned to a downpour. The tent was lighted by a few flaring gas-jets round the central pole, with an opening above them, through which the rain shot down in straight whistling lines. The top of the tent was dripping and saturated, and the gas, shining sideways across, made it glitter in many places with the brilliancy of golden silk. When a sudden squall came with a rush from the narrow valleys behind the town, the whole structure billowed, and flapped and strained, till one waited every moment to see the canvas fall upon our heads. The people, who looked strangely black and swarthy in the uncertain light, were seated all round on three or four rows of raised wooden seats, and many who were late were still crushing forward, and standing in dense masses wherever there was room. At the entrance a rather riotous crowd began to surge in so quickly that there was some danger of the place being rushed. Word was sent across the ring, and in a moment three or four of the women performers, with long streaming ulsters buttoned over their tights, ran out from behind the scenes and threw themselves into the crowd, forcing back the wild hillside people, fishwomen and drunken sailors, in an extraordinary tumult of swearing, wrestling and laughter. These women seemed to enjoy this part of their work, and shrieked with amusement when two or three of them fell on some enormous farmer or publican and nearly dragged him to the ground. Here and there among the people I could see a little party of squireens and their daughters, in the fashions of five years ago, trying, not

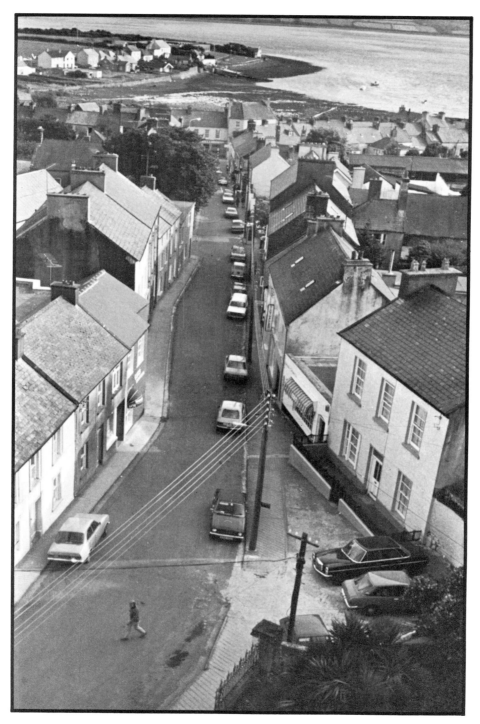

19. *Dingle Town*

always successfully, to reach the shilling seats. The crowd was now so thick I could see little more than the heads of the performers, who had at last come into the ring, and many of the shorter women who were near me must have seen nothing the whole evening, yet they showed no sign of impatience. The performance was begun by the usual dirty white horse, that was brought out and set to gallop round, with a gaudy horse-woman on his back who jumped through a hoop and did the ordinary feats, the horse's hoofs splashing and possing all the time in the green slush of the ring. An old door-mat was laid down near the entrance for the performers, and as they came out in turn they wiped the mud from their feet before they got up on their horses. A little later the clown came out, to the great delight of the people. He was followed by some gymnasts, and then the horse-people came out again in different dress and make-up, and went through their old turns once more. After that there was prolonged fooling between the clown and the chief horseman, who made many mediaeval jokes, that reminded me of little circuses on the outer Boulevards of Paris, and at last the horseman sang a song which won great applause: —

> Here's to the man who kisses his wife,
> And kisses his wife alone;
> For there's many a man kissed another man's wife
> When he thought he kissed his own.

> Here's to the man who rocks his child,
> And rocks his child alone;
> For there's many a man rocked another man's child
> When he thought he rocked his own.

About ten o'clock there seemed to be a lull in the storm, so I went out into the open air with two young men who were going the road I had to travel. The rain had stopped for a moment, but a high wind was blowing as we made our way to a public-house to get a few biscuits and a glass of beer before we started. A sleepy barmaid, who was lolling behind the counter with a novel pricked up her ears when she heard us talking of our journey.

'Surely you are not going to Ballydavid,' she said, 'at such an hour of a night like this.'

We told her we were going to a place which was further away.

'Well,' she said, 'I wouldn't go to that place to-night if you had a coach-and-four to drive me in, and gave me twenty pounds into the bargain! How at all will you get on in the darkness when the roads will be running with water, and you'll be likely to slip down every place into some drain or ditch?'

When we went out, and began to make our way down the steep hill through the town, the night seemed darker than ever after the glare of the bar. Before we had gone many yards a woman's voice called out sharply from under the wall: 'Mind the horse.' I looked up and saw the black outline of a horse's head standing right above me. It was not plain in such darkness how we should get to the end of our ten-mile journey; but one of the young men borrowed a lantern from a chandler in the bottom of the town, and we made our way over the bridge and up the hill, going slowly and painfully with just light enough, when we kept close together, to avoid the sloughs of water and piles of stones on the roadway. By the time we reached the top of the ridge and began to work down carefully towards Smerwick, the rain stopped, and we reached the village without any mishap.

I go out often in the mornings to the site of Sybil Ferriter's Castle, on a little headland reached by a narrow strip of rocks. As I lie there I can watch whole flights of cormorants and choughs and seagulls that fly about under the cliffs, and beyond them a number of niavogues that are nearly always fishing in Ferriter's Cove. Further on there are Sybil Head and three rocky points, the Three Sisters; then Smerwick Harbour and Brandon far away, usually covered with white airy clouds. Between these headlands and the village there is a strip of sandhill grown over with sea-holly, and a low beach where scores of red bullocks lie close to the sea, or wade in above their knees. Further on one passes peculiar horseshoe coves, with contorted lines of sandstone on one side and slaty blue rocks on the other, and necks of transparent sea of wonderful blueness between them.

I walked up this morning along the slope from the east to the top of Sybil Head, where one comes out suddenly on the brow of a cliff with a straight fall of many hundred feet into the sea. It is a place of indescribable grandeur, where one can see Carrantuohill and the Skelligs and Loop Head and the full sweep of the Atlantic, and, over all, the wonderfully tender and searching light that is seen only in Kerry. Looking down the drop of five or six hundred feet, the height is so great that the gannets flying close over the sea look like white butterflies, and the choughs like flies fluttering behind them. One wonders in these places why anyone is left in Dublin, or London, or Paris, when it would be better, one would think, to live in a tent or hut with this magnificent sea and sky, and to breathe this wonderful air, which is like wine in one's teeth.

Here and there on this headland there are little villages of ten or twenty houses, closely packed together without any order or roadway. Usually there are one or two curious beehive-like structures in these villages, used here, it is said, as pig-styes or storehouses. On my way down from Sybil Head I was joined by a tall young man, who told me he had been in the navy, but had bought himself out before his time was over.

'Twelve of us joined from this place,' he said, 'and I was the last of them that stayed in it, for it is a life that no one could put up with. It's not the work that would trouble you, but it's that they can't leave you alone, and that you must be ever and always fooling over something.'

He had been in South Africa during the war, and in Japan, and all over the world; but he was now dressed in homespuns, and had settled down here, he told me, for the rest of his life. Before we reached the village we met Maurice, the fisherman I have spoken of, and we sat down under a hedge to shelter from a shower. We began to talk of fevers and sicknesses and doctors — these little villages are often infested with typhus — and Maurice spoke about the traditional cures.

'There is a plant,' he said, 'which is the richest that is growing out of the ground, and in the old times the women used to be giving it to their children till they'd be growing up seven feet maybe in height. Then the priests and doctors

20. The Bellringer, Dingle

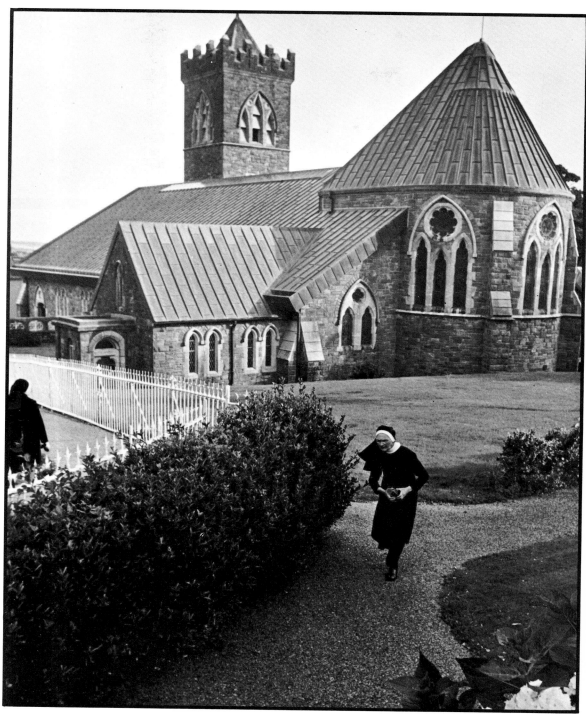

21. St. Mary's Church, Dingle

began taking everything to themselves and destroyed the old knowledge, and that is a poor thing; for you know well it was the Holy Mother of God who cured her own Son with plants the like of that, and said after that no mother should be without a plant for ever to cure her child. Then she threw out the seeds of it over the whole world, so that it's growing every place from that day to this.'

*　　*　　*

I CAME OUT to-day, a holiday, to the Great Blasket Island with a schoolmaster and two young men from the village, who were coming for the afternoon only. The day was admirably clear, with a blue sea and sky, and the voyage in the long canoe — I had not been in one for two or three years — gave me indescribable enjoyment. We passed Dunmore Head, and then stood out nearly due west towards the Great Blasket itself, the height of the mountains round the bay and the sharpness of the rocks making the place singularly different from the sounds about Aran, where I had last travelled in a curagh. As usual, three men were rowing — the man I have come to stay with, his son, and a tall neighbour, all dressed in blue jerseys, home-spun trousers and shirts, and talking in Irish only, though my host could speak good English when he chose to. As we came nearer the island, which seemed to rise like a mountain straight out of the sea, we could make out a crowd of people in their holiday clothes standing or sitting along the brow of the cliff watching our approach, and just beyond them a patch of cottages with roofs of tarred felt. A little later we doubled into a cove among the rocks, where I landed at a boat slip, and then scrambled up a steep zig-zag pathway to the head of the cliff, where the people crowded round us and shook hands with the men who had come with me.

This cottage where I am to stay is one of the highest of the group, and as we passed up to it through little paths among the cottages many white, wolfish-looking dogs came out and barked furiously. My host had gone on in front with my bag, and when I reached his threshold he came forward and shook hands with me again, with a finished speech of welcome. His eldest daughter, a young married woman of about twenty, who manages the house, shook hands with me also, and then, without asking if we were hungry, began making us tea in a metal teapot and frying rashers of bacon. She is a small, beautifully formed woman, with brown hair and eyes — instead of the black hair and blue eyes that are usually found with this type in Ireland — and delicate feet and ankles that are not common in these parts, where the woman's work is so hard. Her sister, who lives in the house also, is a bonny girl of about eighteen, full of humour and spirits.

The schoolmaster made many jokes in English and Irish while the little hostess served our tea; and then the kitchen filled up with young men and women — the men dressed like ordinary fishermen, the women wearing print bodices and coloured skirts, that had none of the distinction of the dress of Aran — and a polka was danced, with curious solemnity, in a whirl of dust. When it was over it was time for my companions to go back to the mainland. As soon as we came out and began

22. Great Blasket Island

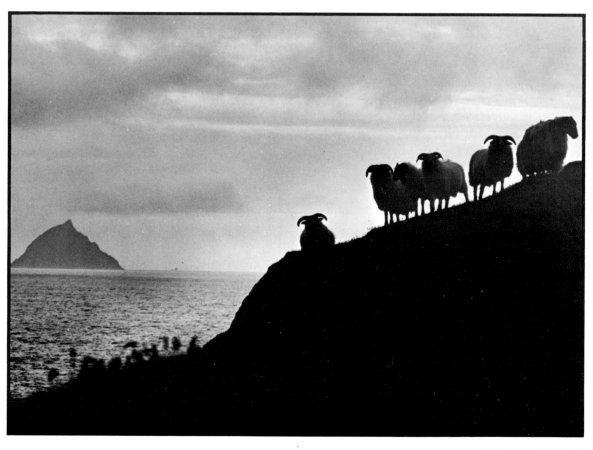

23. *Tearaught Island*

to go down to the sea, a large crowd, made up of nearly all the men and women and children of the island, came down also, closely packed round us. At the edge of the cliff the young men and the schoolmaster bade me good-bye and went down the zig-zag path, leaving me alone with the islanders on the ledge of rock, where I had seen the people as we came in. I sat for a long time watching the sail of the canoe moving away to Dunquin, and talking to a young man who had spent some years in Ballyferriter, and had good English. The evening was peculiarly fine, and after a while, when the crowd had scattered, I passed up through the cottages, and walked through a boreen towards the north-west, between a few plots of potatoes and little fields of weeds that seemed to have gone out of cultivation not long ago. Beyond these I turned up a sharp, green hill, and came out suddenly on the broken edge of a cliff. The effect was wonderful. The Atlantic was right underneath; then I could see the sharp rocks of several uninhabited islands, a mile or two off, the Tearaught further away, and, on my left, the whole northern edge of this island curving round towards the west, with a steep heathery face, a thousand feet high. The whole sight of wild islands and sea was as clear and cold and brilliant as what one sees in a dream, and alive with the singularly severe glory that is in the character of this place.

As I was wandering about I saw many of the younger islanders, not far off, jumping and putting the weight – a heavy stone – or running races on the grass. Then four girls, walking arm-in-arm, came up and talked to me in Irish. Before long they began to laugh loudly at some signs I made to eke out my meaning, and by degrees the men wandered up also, till there was a crowd round us. The cold of the night was growing stronger, however, and we soon turned back to the village, and sat round the fire in the kitchen the rest of the evening.

At eleven o'clock the people got up as one man and went away, leaving me with the little hostess – the man of the house had gone to the mainland with the young men – her husband and sister. I told them I was sleepy, and ready to go to bed; so the little hostess lighted a candle, carried it into the room beyond the kitchen, and stuck it up on the end of the bed-post of one of the beds with a few drops of grease. Then she took off her apron, and fastened it up in the window as a blind, laid another apron on the wet earthen floor for me to stand on, and left me to myself. The room had two beds, running from wall to wall with a small space between them, a chair that the little hostess had brought in, an old hairbrush that was propping the window open, and no other article. When I had been in bed for some time, I heard the host's voice in the kitchen, and a moment or two later he came in with a candle in his hand, and made a long apology for having been away the whole of my first evening on the island, holding the candle while he talked very close to my face. I told him I had been well entertained by his family and neighbours, and had hardly missed him. He went away, and half an hour later opened the door again with the iron spoon which serves to lift the latch, and came in, in a suit of white homespuns, and said he must ask me to let him stretch out in the other bed, as there was no place else for him to lie. I told him that he was welcome, and he got into the other bed and lit his pipe. Then we had a long talk about this place and America and the younger generations.

'There has been no one drowned on this island,' he said, 'for forty years, and that is a great wonder, for it is a dangerous life. There was a man – the brother of the man you were talking to when the girls were dancing — was married to a widow had a public-house away to the west of Ballydavid, and he was out fishing for mackerel, and he got a great haul of them; then he filled his canoe too full, so that she was down to the edge in the water, and a wave broke into her when they were near the shore, and she went down under them. Two men got ashore, but the man from this island was drowned, for his oilskins went down about his feet, and he sank where he was.'

Then we talked about the chances of the mackerel season. 'If the season is good,' he said, 'we get on well; but it is not certain at all. We do pay £4 for a net, and sometimes the dogfish will get into it the first day and tear it into pieces as if you'd cut it with a knife. Sometimes the mackerel will die in the net, and then ten men would be hard set to pull them up into the canoe, so that if the wind rises on us we must cut loose, and let down the net to the bottom of the sea. When we get fish here in the night we go to Dunquin and sell them to buyers in the morning; and, believe me, it is a dangerous thing to cross that sound when you have too great a load taken into your canoe. When it is too bad to cross over we do salt the fish ourselves — we must salt them cleanly and put them in clean barrels — and then the first day it is calm, buyers will be out after them from the town of Dingle.

Afterwards he spoke of the people who go away to America, and the younger generations that are growing up now in Ireland.

'The young people is no use,' he said. 'I am not as good a man as my father was, and my son is growing up worse than I am.' Then he put up his pipe on the end of the bed-post. 'You'll be tired now,' he went on, 'so it's time we were sleeping; and, I humbly beg your pardon, might I ask your name?' I told him.

'Well, good night so,' he said, 'and may you have a good sleep your first night in this island.'

Then he put out the candle and we settled to sleep. In a few minutes I could hear that he was in his dreams, and just as my own ideas were beginning to wander, the house door opened, and the son of the place, a young man of about twenty, came in and walked into our room, close to my bed, with another candle in his hand. I lay with my eyes closed, and the young man did not seem pleased with my presence, though he looked at me with curiosity. When he was satisifed he went back to the kitchen, and took a drink of whisky and said his prayers; then, after loitering about for some time and playing with a little mongrel greyhound that seemed to adore him, he took off his clothes, clambered over his father, and stretched out on the inner side of the bed.

I awoke in the morning about six o'clock, and not long afterwards the host awoke also, and asked how I did. Then he wanted to know if I ever drank whisky; and when he heard that I did so, he began calling for one of his daughters at the top of his voice. In a few moments the younger girl came in, her eyes closing with sleep, and, at the host's bidding, got the whisky bottle, some water, and a green wine-glass out of the kitchen. She came first to my bedside and gave me a dram, then she did the same for her father and brother, handed us our pipes and tobacco, and went back to the kitchen.

There were to be sports at noon in Ballyferriter, and when we had talked for a while I asked the host if he would think well of my going over to see them. 'I would not,' he said; 'you'd do better to stay quiet in this place where you are; the men will be all drunk coming back, fighting and kicking in the canoes, and a man the like of you, who aren't used to us, would be frightened. Then, if you went, the people would be taking you into one public-house, and then into another, till you'd maybe get drunk yourself, and that wouldn't be a nice thing for a gentleman. Stay where you are in this island and you'll be safest so.'

When the son got up later and began going in and out of the kitchen, some of the neighbours, who had already come in, stared at me with curiosity as I lay in my bed; then I got up myself and went into the kitchen. The little hostess set about getting my breakfast, but before it was ready she partly rinsed the dough out of a pan where she had been kneading bread, poured some water into it, and put it on a chair near the door. Then she hunted about the edges of the rafters till she found a piece of soap, which she put on the back of a chair with the towel, and told me I might wash my face. I did so as well as I was able, in the middle of the people, and dried myself with the towel, which was the one used by the whole family.

The morning looked as if it would turn to rain and wind, so I took the advice I had been given and let the canoes go off without me to the sports. After a turn on the cliffs I came back to the house to write letters. The little hostess was washing up the breakfast things when I arrived with my papers and pens, but she made room for me at the table, and spread out an old newspaper for me to write on. A little later, when she had finished her washing, she came over to her usual place in the chimney corner, not far from where I was sitting, sat down on the floor, and took out her hairpins and began combing her hair. As I finished each letter I had to say who it was to, and where the people lived; and then I had to tell her if they were married or single, how many children they had, and make a guess at how many pounds they spent in the year, and at the number of their servants. Just before I finished, the younger girl came back with three or four other young women, who were followed in a little while by a party of men.

I showed them some photographs of the Aran Islands and Wicklow, which they looked at with eagerness. The little hostess was especially taken with two or three that had babies or children in their foreground; and as she put her hands on my shoulders, and leaned over to look at them, with the confidence that is so usual in these places, I could see that she had her full share of passion for children which is powerful in all women who are permanently and profoundly attractive. While I was telling her what I could about the children, I saw one of the men looking with peculiar amazement at an old photograph of myself that had been taken many years ago in an alley of the Luxembourg Gardens, where there were many statues in the background. 'Look at that,' he whispered in Irish to one of the girls, pointing to the statues; 'in those countries they do have naked people standing about in their skins.'

I explained that the figures were of marble only, and then the little hostess and all the girls examined them also. 'Oh! dear me,' said the little hostess, 'Is deas an rud do bheith ag siubhal ins an domhain mor' ('It's a fine thing to be travelling in the big world').

In the afternoon I went up and walked along the narrow central ridge of the island, till I came to the highest point, which is nearly three miles west of the village. The weather was gloomy and wild, and there was something nearly appalling

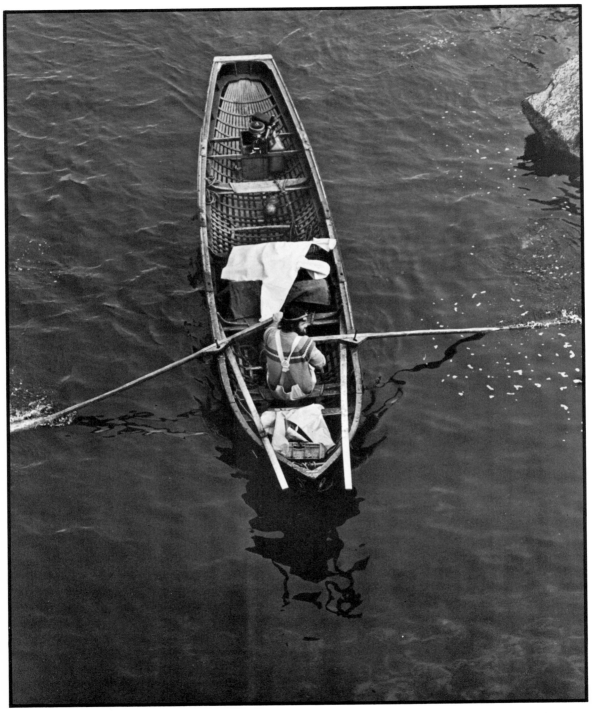

24. Fisherman, Great Blasket Island

in the loneliness of the place. I could look down on either side into a foggy edge of grey moving sea, and then further off I could see many distant mountains, or look out across the shadowy outline of Inishtooskert to the Tearaught rock. While I was sitting on the little mound which marks the summit of the island — a mound stripped and riddled by rabbits — a heavy bank of fog began to work up from the south, behind Valentia, on the other jaw of Dingle Bay. As soon as I saw it I hurried down from the pinnacle where I was, so that I might get away from the more dangerous locality before the cloud overtook me. In spite of my haste I had not gone half a mile when an edge of fog whisked and circled round me, and in a moment I could see nothing but a grey shroud of mist and a few yards of steep, slippery grass. Everything was distorted and magnified to an extraordinary degree; but I could hear the moan of the sea under me, and I knew my direction, so I worked along towards the village without trouble. In some places the island, on this southern side, is bitten into by sharp, narrow coves, and when the fog opened a little I could see across them, where gulls and choughs were picking about on the grass, looking as big as Kerry cattle or black mountain sheep. Before I reached the house the cloud had turned to a sharp shower of rain, and as I went in the water was dripping from my hat. 'Oh! dear me,' said the little hostess, when she saw me, 'Ta tu an-fhluc anois' ('You are very wet now'). She was alone in the house, breathing audibly, with a sort of simple self-importance, as she washed her jugs and teacups. While I was drinking my tea, a little later, some women came in with three or four little girls — the most beautiful children I have ever seen — who live in one of the nearest cottages. They tried to get the little girls to dance a reel together, but the smallest of them went and hid her head in the skirts of the little hostess. In the end two of the little girls danced with two of those who were grown up, to the lilting of one of them. The little hostess sat at the fire while they danced, plucking and drawing a cormorant for the men's dinner, and calling out to the girls when they lost the step of the dance.

In the evenings of Sundays and holidays the young men and girls go out to a rocky headland on the north-west, where there is a long, grassy slope, to dance and amuse themselves; and this evening I wandered out there with two men, telling them ghost stories in Irish as we went. When we turned over the edge of the hill we came on a number of young men lying on the short grass playing cards. We sat down near them, and before long a party of girls and young women came up also and sat down, twenty paces off, on the brink of the cliff, some of them wearing the fawn-coloured shawls that are so attractive and so much thought of in the south. It was just after sunset, and Inishtooskert was standing out with a smoky blue outline against the redness of the sky. At the foot of the cliff a wonderful silvery light was shining on the sea, which already, before the beginning of autumn, was eager and wintry and cold. The little group of blue-coated men lying on the grass, and the group of girls further off, had a singular effect in this solitude of rocks and sea; and in spite of their high spirits it gave me a sort of grief to feel the utter loneliness and desolation of the place that has given these people their finest qualities.

One of the young men had been thrown from a car a few days before on his way home from Dingle, and his face was still raw and bleeding and horrible to look at; but the young girls seemed to find romance in his condition, and several of them went over and sat in a group round him, stroking his arms and face. When the card-playing was over I showed the young men a few tricks and feats, which they worked at themselves, to the great amusement of the girls, till they had accomplished them all. On our way back to the village the young girls ran wild in the twilight, flying and shrieking over the grass, or rushing up behind the young men and throwing them over, if they were able, by a sudden jerk or trip. The men in return caught them by one hand, and spun them round and round four or five times, and then let them go, when they whirled down the grassy slope for many yards, spinning like peg-tops, and only keeping their feet by the greatest efforts or good-luck.

When we got to the village the people scattered for supper, and in our cottage the little hostess swept the floor and sprinkled it with some sand she had brought home in her apron. Then she filled a crock with drinking water, lit the lamp and sat down by the fire to comb her hair. Some time afterwards, when a number of young men had come in, as was usual, to spend the evening, some one said a niavogue was on its way home from the sports. We went out to the door, but it was too dark to see anything except the lights of a little steamer that was passing up the sound, almost beneath us, on its way to Limerick or Tralee. When it had gone by we could hear a furious drunken uproar coming up from a canoe that was somewhere out in the bay. It sounded as if the men were strangling or murdering each other, and it seemed almost miraculous that they should be able to manage their canoe. The people seemed to think they were in no special danger, and we went in again to the fire and talked about porter and whisky (I have never heard the men here talk for half an hour of anything without some allusion to drink), discussing how much a man could drink with comfort in a day, whether it is better to drink when a man is thirsty or at ordinary times, and what food gives the best liking for porter. Then they asked me how much porter I could drink myself, and I told them I could drink whisky, but that I had no taste for porter, and would only take a pint or two at odd times, when I was thirsty.

'The girls are laughing to hear you say that,' said an old man; 'but whisky is a lighter drink, and I'd sooner have it myself, and any old man would say the same.' A little later some young men came in, in their Sunday clothes, and told us the news of the sports.

This morning it was raining heavily, and the host got out some nets and set to work with his son and son-in-law, mending many holes that had been cut by dog-fish, as the mackerel season is soon to begin. While they were at work the kitchen emptied and filled continually with islanders passing in and out, and discussing the weather and the season. Then they started cutting each other's hair, the man who was being cut sitting with an oilskin round him on a little stool by the door, and some other men came in to sharpen their razors on the host's razor-strop, which seems to be the only one on the island. I had not shaved since I arrived, so the little hostess asked me after a while if I would like to shave myself before dinner. I told her I would, so she got me some water in the potato-dish and put it on a chair; then her sister got me a little piece of broken looking-glass and put it on a nail near the door, where there was some light. I set to work, and as I stood with my back to the people I could catch a score of eyes in the glass, watching me intently. 'That is a great improvement to you now,' said the host, when I had done; 'and whenever you want a beard, God bless you, you'll have a thick one surely.'

When I was coming down in the evening from the ridge of the island where I spent much of my time looking at the richness of the Atlantic on one side and the sad or shining greys of Dingle Bay on the other, I was joined by two young women and we walked back together. Just outside the village we met an old woman who stopped and laughed at us. 'Well, aren't you in good fortune this night, stranger,' she said, 'to be walking up and down in the company of women?'

'I am surely,' I answered; 'isn't that the best thing to be doing in the whole world?'

At our own door I saw the little hostess sweeping the floor, so I went down for a moment to the gable of the cottage, and looked out over the roofs of the little village to the sound, where the tide was running with extraordinary force. In a few minutes the little hostess came down and stood beside me — she thought I should not be left by myself when I had been driven away by the dust — and I asked her many questions about the names and relationships of the people that I am beginning to know.

Afterwards, when many of the people had come together in the kitchen, the men told me about their lobster-pots that are brought from Southampton, and cost half-a-crown each. 'In good weather,' said the man who was talking to me, 'they will often last for a quarter; but if storms come up on them they will sometimes break up in a week or two. Still and all, it is a good trade; and we do sell lobsters and crayfish every week in the season to a boat from England or a boat from France that does come in here, as you'll maybe see before you go.'

I told them that I had often been in France, and one of the boys began counting up the numerals in French to show what he had learnt from their buyers. A little later, when the talk was beginning to flag, I turned to a young man near me — the best fiddler, I was told, on the island — and asked him to play us a dance. He made excuses, and would not get his fiddle; but two of the girls slipped off and brought it. The young man tuned it and offered it to me, but I insisted that he should take it first. Then he played one or two tunes, without tone, but with good intonation and rhythm. When it was my turn I played a few tunes also; but the pitch was so low I could not do what I wanted, and I had not much success with the people, though the fiddler himself watched me with interest. 'That is great playing,' he said, when I had finished; 'and I never seen anyone the like of you for moving your hand and getting the sound out of it with the full drag of the bow.' Then he played a polka and four couples danced. The women, as usual, were in their naked feet, and whenever there was a figure for women only there was a curious hush and patter of bare feet, till the heavy pounding and shuffling of the men's boots broke in again. The whirl of music and dancing in this little kitchen stirred me with an extraordinary effect. The kindliness and merrymaking of these islanders, who, one knows, are full of riot and severity and daring, has a quality and attractiveness that is absent altogether from the life of towns, and makes one think of the life that is shown in the ballads of Scotland.

After the dance the host, who had come in, sang a long English doggerel about a poor scholar who went to Maynooth and had great success in his studies, so that he was praised by the bishop. Then he went home for his holiday, and a

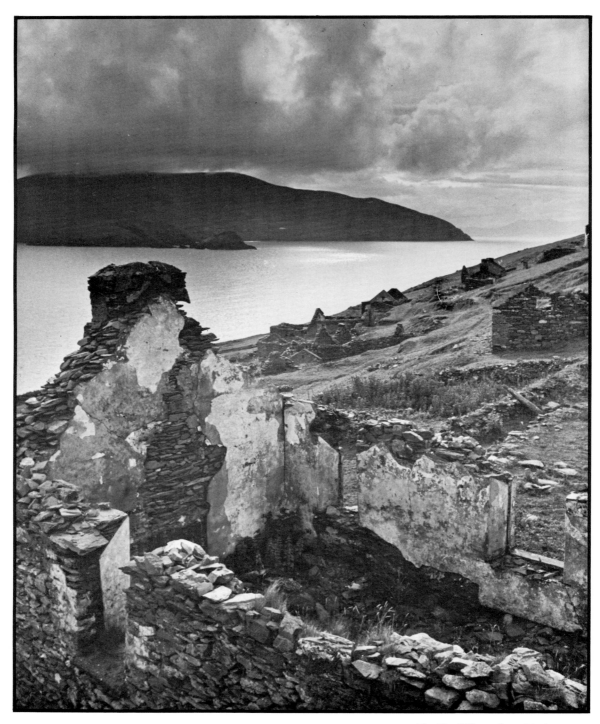

25. *The Village, Great Blasket Island*

young woman who had great riches asked him into her parlour and told him it was no fit life for a fine young man to be a priest, always saying Mass for poor people, and that he would have a right to give up his Latin and get married to herself. He refused her offers and went back to his college. When he was gone she went to the justice in great anger, and swore an oath against him that he had seduced her and left her with child. He was brought back for his trial, and he was in risk to be degraded and hanged, when a man rode up on a horse and said it was himself was the lover of the lady, and the father of her child.

Then they told me about an old man of eighty years, who is going to spend the winter alone on Inishvickillaun, an island six miles from this village. His son is making canoes and doing other carpenter's jobs on this island, and the other children have scattered also; but the old man refuses to leave the island he has spent his life on, so they have left him with a goat, and a bag of flour and stack of turf.

I have just been to the weaver's, looking at his loom and appliances. The host took me down to his cottage over the brow of the village, where some young men were finishing the skeleton of a canoe; and we found his family crowded round a low table on green stools with rope seats, finishing their dinner of potatoes. A little later the old weaver, who looks pale and sickly compared with the other islanders, took me into a sort of outhouse with a damp feeling in the air, where his loom was set up. He showed me how it was worked, and then brought out some pieces of stuff that he had woven. At first I was puzzled by the fine brown colour of some of the material; but they explained it was from selected wools of the black or mottled sheep that are common here, and are so variegated that many tints of grey or brown can be had from their fleeces. The wool for the flannel is sometimes spun on this island; sometimes it is given to women in Dunquin, who spin it cheaply for so much a pound. Then it is woven, and finally the stuff is sent to a mill in Dingle to be cleaned and dressed before it is given to a tailor in Dingle to be made up for their own use. Such cloth is not cheap, but is of wonderful quality and strength. When I came out of the weaver's, a little sailing smack was anchored in the sound, and someone on board her was blowing a horn. They told me she was the French boat, and as I went back to my cottage I could see many canoes hurrying out to her with their cargoes of lobsters and crabs.

I have left the island again. I walked round the cliffs in the morning, and then packed my bag in my room, several girls putting their heads into the little window while I did so, to say it was a great pity I was not staying on for another week or a fortnight. Then the men went off with my bag in a heavy shower, and I waited a minute or two while the little hostess buttered some bread for my lunch, and tied it up in a clean handkerchief of her own. Then I bid them good-bye, and set off down to the slip with three girls, who came with me to see that I did not go astray among the innumerable paths. It was still raining heavily, so I told them to put my cape, which they were carrying, over their heads. They did so with delight, and ran down the path before me, to the great amusement of the islanders. At the head of the cliff many people were standing about to bid me goodbye and wish me a good voyage.

The wind was in our favour, so the men took in their oars after rowing for about a quarter of a mile and lay down in the bottom of the canoe, while one man ran up the sail, and the host steered with an oar. At Dunquin the host hired me a dray, without springs, kissed my hand in farewell, and I was driven away.

* * *

I HAVE MADE my way round the foot of Dingle Bay and up the south coast to a cottage where I often lodge. As I was resting in a ditch sometime in the afternoon, on a lonely mountain road, a little girl came along with a shawl over her head. She stopped in front of me and asked me where I was going, and then after a little talk: 'Well, man, let you come,' she said; 'I'm going your road as well as you.' I got up and we started. When I got tired of the hill I mounted, and she ran along beside me for several miles, till we fell in with some people cutting turf, and she stopped to talk to them.

Then for a while my road ran round an immense valley of magnificent rich turf bog, with mountains all round, and bowls where hidden lakes were lying bitten out of the cliffs.

As I was resting again on a bridge over the Behy where Diarmuid caught salmon with Grania, a man stopped to light his pipe and talk to me. 'There are three lakes above,' he said, 'Coomacarra, Coomaglaslaw and Coomasdhara; the whole of this place was in a great state in the bad times. Twenty years ago they sent down a 'mergency man to lodge above by the lake and serve processes on the people, but the people were off before him and lay abroad in the heather. Then, in the course of a piece, a night came, with great rain out of the heavens, and my man said: "I'll get them this night in their own beds, surely." Then he let call the peelers — they had peelers waiting to mind him — and down they come to the big stepping-stones they have above for crossing the first river coming out of the lakes. My man going in front to cross over, and the water was high up covering the stones. Then he gave two leps or three, and the peelers heard him give a great shriek down in the flood. They went home after — what could they do? — and the 'mergency man was found in the sea stuck in a net.'

I was singularly pleased when I turned up the boreen at last to this cottage where I lodge, and looked down through a narrow gully to Dingle Bay. The people bade me welcome when I came in, the old woman kissing my hand.

There is no village near this cottage, yet many farms are scattered on the hills near it; and as the people are in some ways a leading family, many men and women look in to talk or tell stories, or to buy a few pennyworth of sugar or starch. Although the main road passes a few hundred yards to the west, this cottage is well known also to the race of local tramps who move from one family to another in some special neighbourhood or barony. This evening, when I came in, a little old man in a tall hat and long brown coat was sitting up on the settle beside the fire, and intending to spend, one could see, a night or more in the place.

I had a great deal to tell the people at first of my travels in different parts of

86

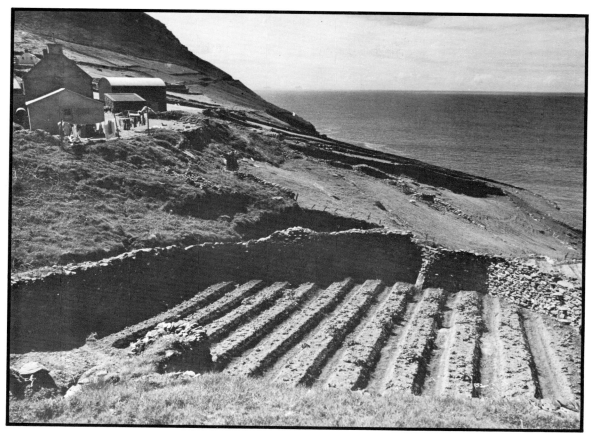

26. Coumeenoole, Dingle Peninsula

the county, to the Blasket Islands — which they can see from here — Corkaguiney and Tralee; and they had news to tell me also of people who have married or died since I was here before, or gone away, or come back from America. Then I was told that the old man, Dermot (or Darby, as he is called in English), was the finest story-teller in Iveragh; and after a while he told us a long story in Irish, but spoke so rapidly and indistinctly — he had no teeth — that I could understand but few passages. When he had finished I asked him where he had heard the story.

'I heard it in the city of Portsmouth,' he said. 'I worked there for fifteen years, and four years in Plymouth, and a long while in the hills of Wales; twenty-five years in all I was working at the other side; and there were many Irish in it, who would be telling stories in the evening, the same as we are doing here. I heard many good stories, but what can I do with them now and I an old lisping fellow, the way I can't give them out like a ballad?'

When he had talked a little more about his travels, and a bridge over the Severn, that he thought the greatest wonder of the world, I asked him if he remembered the Famine.

'I do,' he said. 'I was living near Kenmare, and many's the day I saw them burying the corpses in the ditch by the road. It was after that I went to England, for this country was ruined and destroyed. I heard there was work at that time in Plymouth; so I went to Dublin and took a boat that was going to England; but it was at a place called Liverpool they put me on shore, and then I had to walk to Plymouth, asking my way on the road. In that place I saw the soldiers after coming back from the Crimea, and they all broken and maimed.'

A little later, when he went out for a moment, the people told me he beats up and down between Killorglin and Ballinskelligs and the Inny river, and that he is a particular crabby kind of man, and will not take anything from the people but coppers and eggs.

'And he's a wasteful old fellow with all,' said the woman of the house, 'though he's eighty years old or beyond it, for whatever money he'll get one day selling his eggs to the coastguards, he'll spend it the next getting a drink when he's thirsty, or keeping good boots on his feet.'

From that they began talking of misers, and telling stories about them.

'There was an old woman,' said one of the men, 'living beyond to the east, and she was thought to have a great store of money. She had one daughter only, and in the course of a piece a young lad got married to her, thinking he'd have her fortune. The woman died after — God be merciful to her! — and left the two of them as poor as they were before. Well, one night a man that knew them was passing to the fair of Puck, and he came in and asked would they give him a lodging for that night. They gave him what they had and welcome and after his tea, when they were sitting over the fire — the way we are this night — the man asked them how they were so poor-looking, and if the old woman had left nothing behind her.

' "Not a farthing did she leave," said the daughter.

' "And did she give no word or warning or message in her last moments?" said the man.

' "She did not," said the daughter, "except only that I shouldn't comb out the hair of her poll and she dead."

' "And you heeded her?" said the man.

27. *Caha Mountains*

' "I did, surely," said the daughter.

' "Well," said the man, "to-morrow night when I'm gone let the two of you go down the Relic (the graveyard) and dig up her coffin and look in her hair and see what it is you'll find in it."

' "We'll do that," said the daughter, and with that they all stretched out for the night.

'The next evening they went down quietly with a shovel and they dug up the coffin, and combed through her hair, and there behind her poll they found her fortune, five hundred pounds, in good notes and gold.'

'There was an old fellow living on the little hill beyond the graveyard,' said Dannyboy, when the man had finished, 'and he had his fortune some place hid in his bed, and he was an old weak fellow, so that they were all watching him to see he wouldn't hide it away. One time there was no one in it but himself and a young girl, and the old fellow slipped out of his bed and went out of the door as far as a little bush and some stones. The young girl kept her eye on him, and she made sure he'd hidden something in the bush; so when he was back in his bed she called the people, and they all came and looked in the bushes, but not a thing could they find. The old man died after, and no one ever found his fortune to this day.'

'There were some young lads a while since,' said the old woman, 'and they went up of a Sunday and began searching through those bushes to see if they could find anything, but a kind of a turkey-cock came up out of the stones and drove them away.'

'There was another old woman,' said the man of the house, 'who tried to take down her fortune into her stomach. She was near death, and she was all day stretched in her bed at the corner of the fire. One day when the girl was tinkering about, the old woman rose up and got ready a little skillet that was near the hob and put something into it and put it down by the fire, and the girl watching her all the time under her oxter, not letting on she seen her at all. When the old woman lay down again the girl went over to put on more sods on the fire, and she got a look into the skillet, and what did she see but sixty sovereigns. She knew well what the old woman was striving to do, so she went out to the dairy and she got a lump of fresh butter and put it down into the skillet, when the woman didn't see her do it at all. After a bit the old woman rose up and looked into the skillet, and when she saw the froth of the butter she thought it was the gold that was melted. She got back into her bed — a dark place, maybe — and she began sipping and sipping the butter till she had the whole of it swallowed. Then the girl made some trick to entice the skillet away from her, and she found the sixty sovereigns in the bottom and she kept them for herself.'

By this time it was late, and the old woman brought over a mug of milk and a piece of bread to Darby at the settle, and the people gathered at their table for their supper; so I went into the little room at the end of the cottage where I am given a bed.

When I came into the kitchen in the morning, old Darby was still asleep on the settle, with his coat and trousers over him, a red night-cap on his head, and his half-bred terrier, Jess, chained with a chain he carries with him to the leg of the settle.

'That's a poor way to lie on the bare board,' said the woman of the house, when she saw me looking at him; 'but when I filled a sack with straw for him last

90

night he wouldn't have it at all.'

While she was boiling some eggs for my breakfast, Darby roused up from his sleep, pulled on his trousers and coat, slipped his feet into his boots and started off, when he had eaten a few mouthfuls, for another house where he is known, some five miles away.

Afterwards I went out on the cnuceen, a little hill between this cottage and the sea, to watch the people gathering carragheen moss, a trade which is much followed in this district during the spring tides of summer. I lay down on the edge of the cliff, where the heathery hill comes to an end and the steep rocks begin. About a mile to the west there was a long headland, 'Feakle Callaigh' ('The Witch's Tooth'), covered with mists, that blew over me from time to time with a swish of rain, followed by sunshine again. The mountains on the other side of the bay were covered, so I could see nothing but the strip of brilliant sea below me, thronged with girls and men up to their waists in the water, with a hamper in one hand and a stick in the other, gathering the moss, and talking and laughing loudly as they worked. The long frill of dark golden rocks covered with seaweed, with the asses and children slipping about on it, and the bars of silvery light breaking through on the further inlets of the bay, had the singularly brilliant liveliness one meets everywhere in Kerry.

When the tide began to come in I went down one of the passes to the sea, and met many parties of girls and old men and women coming up with what they had gathered, most of them still wearing the clothes that had been in the sea, and were heavy and black with salt water. A little further on I met Danny-boy and we sat down to talk.

'Do you see that sandy head?' he said, pointing out to the east, 'that is called the Stooks of the Dead Women; for one time a boat came ashore there with twelve dead women on board her, big ladies with green dresses and gold rings, and fine jewelries, and a dead harper or fiddler along with them. Then there are graves again in the little hollow by the cnuceen, and what we call them is the Graves of the Sailors; for some sailors, Greeks or great strangers, were washed in there a hundred years ago, and it is there that they were buried.'

Then we began talking of the carragheen he had gathered and the spring-tides that would come again during the summer. I took out my diary to tell him the times of the moon, but he would hardly listen to me. When I stopped, he gave his ass a cut with his stick, 'Go on, now,' he said; 'I wouldn't believe those almanacks at all; they do not tell the truth about the moon.'

* * *

THE GREATEST event in West Kerry is the horse-fair, known as Puck Fair, which is held in August. If one asks anyone, many miles east or west of Killorglin, when he reaped his oats or sold his pigs or heifers, he will tell you it was four or five weeks, or whatever it may be, before or after Puck. On the main roads, for many days past, I have been falling in with tramps and trick characters of all kinds, sometimes single and sometimes in parties of four or five, and as I am on the roads a great deal I have often met the same persons several days in succession — one day perhaps at Ballinskelligs, the next day at Feakle Callaigh, and the third in the outskirts of Killorglin.

Yesterday cavalcades of every sort were passing from the west with droves of horses, mares, jennets, foals and asses, with their owners going after them in flat or railed carts, or riding on ponies.

The men of this house — they are going to buy a horse — went to the fair last night, and I followed at an early hour in the morning. As I came near Killorglin the road was much blocked by the latest sellers pushing eagerly forward, and early purchasers who were anxiously leading off their young horses before the roads became dangerous from the crush of drunken drivers and riders.

Just outside the town, near the first public-house, blind beggars were kneeling on the pathway, praying with almost Oriental volubility for the souls of anyone who would throw them a coin.

'May the Holy Immaculate Mother of Jesus Christ,' said one of them, 'intercede for you in the hour of need. Relieve a poor blind creature, and may Jesus Christ relieve yourselves in the hour of death. May He have mercy, I'm saying, on your brothers and fathers and sisters for evermore.'

Further on stalls were set out with cheap cakes and refreshments, and one could see that many houses had been arranged to supply the crowds who had come in. Then I came to the principal road that goes round the fair-green, where there was a great concourse of horses, trotting and walking and galloping; most of them were of the cheaper class of animal, and were selling, apparently to the people's satisfaction, at prices that reminded one of the time when fresh meat was sold for three pence a pound. At the further end of the green there were one or two rough shooting galleries, and a number of women — not very rigid, one could see — selling, or appearing to sell, all kinds of trifles: a set that come in, I am told, from towns not far away. At the end of the green I turned past the chapel, where a little crowd had just carried in a man who had been killed or badly wounded by a fall from a horse, and went down to the bridge of the river, and then back again into the main slope of the town. Here there were a number of people who had come in for amusement only, and were walking up and down, looking at each other — a crowd is as exciting as champagne to these lonely people, who live in long glens among the mountains — and meeting with cousins and friends. Then, in the three-cornered space in the middle of the town, I came on Puck himself, a magnificent he-goat (Irish puc), raised on a platform twenty feet high, and held by a chain from each horn, with his face down the road. He is kept in this position, with a few cabbages to feed on, for three days, so that he may preside over the pig-fair and the horse-fair and the day of winding up.

At the foot of this platform, where the crowd was thickest, a young ballad-singer was howling a ballad in honour of Puck, making one think of the early Greek festivals, since the time of which, it is possible, the goat has been exalted yearly in Killorglin.

The song was printed in on a green slip by itself. It ran: —

28. *Puck Fair, Killorglin*

A NEW SONG ON THE GREAT PUCK FAIR
by John Purcell

All young lovers that are fond of sporting, pay attention for a while,
I will sing you the praises of Puck Fair, and I'm sure it will make you smile;
Where the lads and lassies coming gaily to Killorglin can be seen,
To view the Puck upon the stage, as our hero dressed in green.

Chorus.

And hurra for the gallant Puck so gay,
For he is a splendid one:
Wind and rain don't touch his tail,
For his hair is thirty inches long.

Now it is on the square he's erected with all colours grand and gay;
There's not a fair throughout Ireland, but Puck Fair it takes the sway,
Where you see the gamblers in rotation, trick-o'-the-loop and other games,
The ballad-singers and the wheel-of-fortune and the shooting-gallery for to take aim.

Chorus.

Where is the tyrant dare oppose it?
Our old customs we will hold up still,
And I think we will have another —
That is, Home Rule and Purchase Bill.

Now, all young men that are not married, next Shrove can take a wife,
For before next Puck Fair we will have Home Rule,
and then you will be settled down in life.
Now the same advice I give young girls for to get married and have pluck.
Let the landlords see that you defy them when coming to Fair of Puck.

Céad Míle Fáilte to the Fair of Puck.

29. *Tin Whistle Player*

When one makes the obvious elisions, the lines are not so irregular as they look, and are always sung to a measure; yet the whole, in spite of the assonance, rhymes, and the 'colours grand and gay' seem pitifully remote from any good spirit of ballad-making.

Across the square, a man and a woman, who had a baby tied on her back, were singing another ballad on the Russian and Japanese War, in the curious method of antiphony that is still sometimes heard in the back streets of Dublin. These are some of the verses: —

Man.

Now provisions are rising, 'tis sad for to state,

The flour, tea and sugar, tobacco and meat;

But God help us! poor Irish, how we must stand the test

Ambo.

If they only now stop the trade of commerce.

Woman.

Now the Russians are powerful on sea and on land;

But the Japs they are active, they will them command,

Before this war is finished I have one word to say,

Ambo.

There will be more shot and drowned than in the Crimea.

Man.

Now the Japs are victorious up to this time,

And thousands of Russians I hear they are dying.

Etc., etc.

And so it went on with the same alternation of the voices through seven or eight verses; and it was curious to feel how much was gained by this simple variation of the voices.

When I passed back to the fair-green, I met the men I am staying with, and went off with them under an archway, and into a back yard to look at a little two-year-old filly that they had bought and left for the moment in a loose box with three or four young horses. She was prettily and daintily shaped, but looked too light, I thought, for the work she will be expected to do. As we came out again into the road, an old man was singing an out-spoken ballad on women in the middle of the usual crowd. Just as we passed it came to a scandalous conclusion; and the women scattered in every direction, shrieking with laughter and holding shawls over their mouths.

At the corner we turned into a public-house where there were men we knew, who had done their business also; and we went into the little alcove to sit down quietly for a moment. 'What will you take, sir;' said the man I lodge with, 'a glass of wine?'

I took beer and the others took porter; but we were only served after some little time, as the house was thronged with people.

The men were too much taken up with their bargains and losses to talk much of other matters; and before long we came out again, and the son of the house started homewards, leading the new filly by a little halter of rope.

Not long afterwards I started also. Outside Killorglin rain was coming up over the hills of Glen Car, so that there was a strained hush in the air, and a rich, aromatic smell coming from the bog myrtle, or boggy shrub, that grows thickly in this place. The strings of horses and jennets scattered over the road did not keep away a strange feeling of loneliness that seems to hang over this brown plain of bog that stretches from Carrantuohill to Cuchulain's House.

Before I reached the cottage dense torrents or rain were closing down through the glens, and driving in white sheets between the little hills that are on each side of the way.

* * *

ONE MORNING in autumn I started in a local train for the first stage of my journey to Dublin, seeing the last of Macgillicuddy's Reeks, that were touched with snow in places, Dingle Bay and the islands beyond it. At a little station where I changed trains, I got into a carriage where there was a woman with her daughter, a girl of about twenty, who seemed uneasy and distressed. Soon afterwards, when a collector was looking at our tickets, I called out that mine was for Dublin, and as soon as he got out the woman came over to me.

'Are you going to Dublin?' she said.

I told her I was.

'Well,' she went on, 'here is my daughter going there too; and maybe you'd look after her, for I'm getting down at the next station. She is going up to a hospital for some little complaint in her ear, and she has never travelled before, so that she's lonesome in her mind.'

I told her I would do what I could, and at the next station I was left alone with my charge, and one other passenger, a returned American girl, who was on her way to Mallow, to get the train for Queenstown. When her mother was lost sight of the young girl broke out into tears, and the returned American and myself had trouble to quiet her.

'Look at me,' said the American. 'I'm going off for ten years to America, all by myself, and I don't care a rap.'

When the girl got quiet again, the returned American talked to me about scenery and politics and the arts — she had been seen off by her sisters in bare feet, with shawls over their heads — and the life of women in America.

At several stations girls and boys thronged in to get places for Queenstown, learing parties of old men and women wailing with anguish on the platform. At one place an old woman was seized with such a passion of regret, when she saw her daughters moving away from her for ever, that she made a wild rush after the train; and when I looked out for a moment I could see her writhing and struggling on the platform, with her hair over her face, and two men holding her by the arms.

Two young men had got into our compartment for a few stations only, and they looked on with the greatest satisfaction.

'Ah,' said one of them, 'we do have great sport every Friday and Saturday, seeing the old women howling in the stations.'

When we reached Dublin I left my charge for a moment to see after my baggage, and when I came back I found her sitting on a luggage barrow, with her package in her hand, crying with despair because several cabmen had refused to let her into their cabs, on the pretext that they dreaded infection.

I could see they were looking out for some rich tourist with his trunks, as a more lucrative fare; so I sent for the head-porter, who had charge of the platform. When the porter arrived we chose a cab, and I saw my charge driven off to her hospital, sitting on the front seat, with her handkerchief to her eyes.

*   *   *

FOR THE last few days — I am staying in the Kerry cottage I have spoken of already — the people have been talking of horse-races that were to be held on the sand, not far off, and this morning I set out to see them with the man and woman of the house and two of their neighbours. Our way led through a steep boreen for a quarter of a mile to the edge of the sea, and then along a pathway between the cliffs and a straight grassy hill. When we had gone some distance the old man pointed out a slope in front of us, where, he said, Diarmuid had done his tricks of rolling the barrel and jumping over his spear, and had killed many of his enemies. He told me the whole story, slightly familiarized in detail, but not very different from the version everyone knows. A little further on he pointed across the sea to our left — just beyond the strand where the races were to be run — to a neck of sand where, he said, Oisin was called away to the Tir-na-nOg.

'The Tir-na-nOg itself,' he said, 'is below that sea, and a while since there were two men out in a boat in the night-time, and they got stuck outside some way or another. They went to sleep then, and when one of them wakened up he looked down into the sea, and he saw the Tir-na-Nog and people walking about, and side-cars driving in the squares.'

Then he began telling me stories of mermaids — a common subject in this neighbourhood.

'There was one time a man beyond of the name of Shee,' he said, 'and his master seen a mermaid on the sand beyond combing her hair, and he told Shee to get her. "I will," said Shee, "if you'll give me the best horse you have in your stable." "I'll do that," said the master. Then Shee got the horse, and when he

98

30. Valentia Island

saw the mermaid on the sand combing her hair, with her covering laid away from her, he galloped up, when she wasn't looking, and he picked up the covering and away he went with it. Then the waves rose up behind him and he galloped his best, and just as he was coming out at the top of the tide the ninth wave cut off his horse behind his back, and left himself and the half of his horse and the covering on the dry land. Then the mermaid came in after her covering, and the master got married to her, and she lived with him a long time, and had children — three or four of them. Well, in the wind-up, the master built a fine new house, and when he was moving into it, and clearing the things out, he brought down an old hamper out of the loft and put it in the yard. The woman was going about, and she looked into the hamper, and she saw her covering hidden away in the bottom of it. She took it out then and put it upon her and went back into the sea, and her children used to be on the shore crying after her. I'm told from that day there isn't one of the Shees can go out in a boat on that bay and not be drowned.'

We were now near the sandhills, where a crowd was beginning to come together, and booths were being put up for the sale of apples and porter and cakes. A train had come in a little before at a station a mile or so away, and a number of the usual trick-characters, with their stock-in-trade, were hurrying down to the sea. The roulette man passed us first, unfolding his table and calling out at the top of his voice:

Come play me a game of timmun and tup,
The more you puts down the more you takes up.

'Take notice, gentlemen, I come here to spend a fortune, not to make one. Is there any sportsman in a hat or a cap, or a wig or a waistcoat, will play a go with me now? Take notice, gentlemen, the luck is on the green.'

The races had to be run between two tides while the sand was dry, so there was not much time to be lost, and before we reached the strand the horses had been brought together, ridden by young men in many variations of jockey dress. For the first race there was one genuine race-horse, very old and bony, and two or three young horses belonging to farmers in the neighbourhood. The start was made from the middle of the crowd at the near end of the strand, and the course led out along the edge of the sea to a post some distance away, back again to the starting-point, round a post, and out and back once more.

When the word was given the horses set off in a wild helter-skelter along the edge of the sea, with crowds cheering them on from the sandhills. As they got small in the distance it was not easy to see which horse was leading, but after a sort of check, as they turned the post, they began nearing again a few yards from the waves, with the old race-horse, heavily pressed, a good length ahead. The stewards made a sort of effort to clear the post that was to be circled, but without much success, as the people were wild with excitement. A moment later the old race-horse galloped into the crowd, twisted too suddenly, something cracked and jolted, and it limped out on three legs, gasping with pain. The next horse could not be stopped, and galloped out at the wrong end of the crowd for some little way before it could be brought back, so the last horses set off in front for the final lap.

The lame race-horse was now mobbed by onlookers and advisers, talking incoherently.

100

'Was it the fault of the jock?' said one man.

'It was not,' said another, 'for Michael (the owner) did't strike him, and if it had been his fault, wouldn't he have broken his bones?'

'He was striving to spare a young girl had run out in his way,' said another. 'It was for that he twisted him.'

'Little slut!' said a woman; 'what did she want beyond on the sand?'

Many remedies were suggested that did not sound reassuring, and in the end the horse was led off in a hopeless condition. A little later the race ended with an easy win for the wildest of the young horses. Afterwards I wandered up among the people, and looked at the sports. At one place a man, with his face heavily blackened, except one cheek and eye — an extraordinary effect — was standing shots of a wooden ball behind a board with a large hole in the middle, at three shots a penny. When I came past half an hour afterwards he had been hit in the mouth — by a girl some one told me — but seemed as cheerful as ever.

On the road, some little distance away, a party of girls and young men were dancing polkas to the music of a melodeon, in a cloud of dust. When I had looked on for a little while I met some girls I knew, and asked them how they were getting on.

'We're not getting on at all,' said one of them, 'for we've been at the races for two hours, and we've found no beaux to go along with us.'

When the horses had all run, a jennet race was held, and greatly delighted the people, as the jennets — there were a number of them — got scared by the cheering and ran wild in every direction. In the end it was not easy to say which was the winner, and a dispute began which nearly ended in blows. It was decided at last to run the race over again the following Sunday after Mass, so everyone was satisfied.

The day was magnificently bright, and the ten miles of Dingle Bay were wonderfully brilliant behind the masses of people, and the canvas booths, and the scores of upturned shafts. Towards evening I got tired taking or refusing the porter my friends pressed on me continually, so I wandered off from the racecourse along the path where Diarmuid had tricked the Fenians.

Later in the evening news had been coming in of the doings in the sandhills, after the porter had begun to take effect and the darkness had come on.

'There was great sport after you left,' a man said to me in the cottage this evening. 'They were all beating and cutting each other on the shore of the sea. Four men fought together in one place till the tide came up on them, and was like to drown them; but the priest waded out up to his middle and drove them asunder. Another man was left for dead on the road outside the lodges, and some gentleman found him and had him carried into his house, and got the doctor to put plasters on his head. Then there was a red-headed fellow had his finger bitten through, and the postman was destroyed for ever.'

'He should be,' said the man of the house, 'for Michael Patch broke the seat of his car into three halves on his head.'

'It was this was the cause of it all,' said Danny-boy: 'they brought in porter east and west from the two towns you know of, and the two porters didn't agree together, and it's for that the people went raging at the fall of night.'

31. Beara Peninsula

I HAVE been out to Bolus Head, one of the finest places I have met with. A little beyond Ballinskelligs the road turns up the side of a steep mountainy hill where one sees a brilliant stretch of sea, with many rocks and islands — Deenish, Scariff, the Hog's Head, and Dursey far away. As I was sitting on the edge of the road an old man came along and we began to talk. He had little English, but when I tried him in Irish we got on well, though he did not follow any Connaught forms I let slip by accident. We went on together, after a while, to an extraordinary straggling village along the edge of the hill. At one of the cottages he stopped and asked me to come in and take a drink and rest myself. I did not like to refuse him, we had got so friendly, so I followed him in, and sat down on a stool while his wife — a much younger woman — went into the bedroom and brought me a large mug of milk. As I was drinking it and talking to the couple, a sack that was beside the fire began to move slowly, and the head of a yellow, feverish-looking child came out from beneath it, and began looking at me with a heavy stare. I asked the woman what ailed it, and she told me it had sickened a night or two before with headache and pains all through it; but she had not had the doctor, and did not know what was the matter. I finished the milk without much enjoyment, and went on my way up Bolus Head and then back to this cottage, wondering all the time if I had the germs of typhus in my blood.

Last night, when I got back to the cottage, I found that another 'travelling man' had arrived to stay for a day or two; but he was hard of hearing and a little simple in his head, so that we had not much talk. I went to bed soon after dark and slept till about two o'clock in the morning, when I was awakened by fearful screams in the kitchen. For a moment I did not know where I was; then I remembered the old man, and I jumped up and went to the door of my room. As I opened it I heard the door of the family room across the kitchen opening also, and the frightened whispers of the people. In a moment we could hear the old man, who was sleeping on the settle, pulling himself out of a nightmare, so we went back to our beds.

In the morning the woman told me his story: —

'He was living above on a little hillside,' she said, 'in a bit of a cabin, with his sister along with him. Then, after a while, she got ailing in her heart, and he got a bottle for her from the doctor, and he'd rise up every morning before the dawn to give her a sup of it. She got better then, till one night he got up and measured out the spoonful, or whatever it was, and went to give it to her, and he found her stretched out dead before him. Since that night he wakes up one time and another, and begins crying out for Maurya — that was his sister — and he half in his dreams. It was that you heard in the night, and indeed it would frighten any person to hear him screaming as if he was getting his death.'

When the little man came back after a while, they began asking him questions till he told his whole story, weeping pitiably. Then they got him to tell me about the other great event of his life also, in the rather childish Gaelic he uses.

He had once a little cur-dog, he said, and he knew nothing of the dog licence; then one day the peelers — the boys with the little caps — asked him into the barracks for a cup of tea. He went in cheerfully, and then they put him and his little dog into the lock-up till some one paid a shilling for him and got him out.

He has a stick he is proud of, bound with pieces of leather every few inches — like one I have seen with a beggar in Belmullet. Since the first night he has not had nightmare again, and he lies most of the evening sleeping on the settle, and in the morning he goes round among the houses, getting his share of meal and potatoes.

I do not think a beggar is ever refused in Kerry. Sometimes, while we are talking or doing something in the kitchen, a man walks in without saying anything and stands just inside the door, with his bag on the floor beside him. In five or ten minutes, when the woman of the house has finished what she is doing, she goes up to him and asks: 'Is it meal or flour?' 'Flour,' says the man. She goes into the inner room, opens her sack, and comes back with two handfuls. He opens his bag and takes out a bundle carefully tied up in a cloth or handkerchief; he opens this again, and usually there is another cloth inside, into which the woman puts her flour. Then the cloths are carefully knotted together by the corners, put back in the bag, and the man mutters a 'God bless you,' and goes on his way.

The meal, flour and potatoes that are thus gathered up are always sold by the beggar, and the money is spent on porter or second-hand clothes, or very occasionally on food when he is in a neighbourhood that is not hospitable. The buyers are usually found among the coastguards' wives, or in the little public-house on the roadside.

'Some of these men,' said the woman of the house, when I asked her about them, 'will take their flour nicely and tastily and cleanly, and others will throw it in anyway, and you'd be sorry to eat it afterwards.'

The talk of these people is almost bewildering. I have come to this cottage again and again, and I often think I have heard all they have to say, and then some one makes a remark that leads to a whole new bundle of folk-tales, or stories of wonderful events that have happened in the barony in the last hundred years. To-night the people were unusually silent, although several neighbours had come in, and to make conversation I said something about the bull-fights in Spain that I had been reading of in the newspapers. Immediately they started off with stories of wicked or powerful bulls, and then they branched off to clever dogs and all the things they have done in West Kerry, and then to mad dogs and mad cattle and pigs — one incident after another, but always detailed and picturesque and interesting.

*　*　*

I HAVE come back to the north of Dingle, leaving Tralee late in the afternoon. At the station there was a more than usually great crowd, as there had been a fair in the town and many people had come in to make their Saturday purchases. A number of messenger boys with parcels from the shops in the town were shouting for the owners, using many familiar names, Justin MacCarthy, Hannah Lynch and the like. I managed to get a seat on a sack of flour beside the owner, who had other

32. Green Street, Dingle

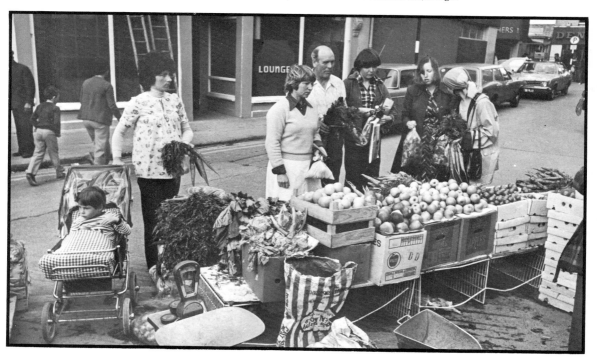

33. Tralee Market

105

packages scattered under our feet. When the train had started and the women and girls — the carriage was filled with them — had settled down into their places, I could see I caused great curiosity, as it was too late in the year for even an odd tourist, and on this line everyone is known by sight.

Before long I got into talk with the old man next me, and as soon as I did so the women and girls stopped their talk and leaned out to hear what we were saying.

He asked first if I belonged to Dingle, and I told him I did not.

'Well,' he says, 'you speak like a Kerry man, and you're dressed like a Kerry man, so you belong to Kerry surely.'

I told him I was born and bred in Dublin, and that I had travelled in many places in Ireland and beyond it.

'That's easy said,' he answered, 'but I'd take an oath you were never beyond Kerry to this day.' Then he asked sharply: — 'What do you do?'

I answered something about my wanderings in Europe, and suddenly he sat up, as if a new thought had come to him.

'Maybe you're a wealthy man?' he said. I smiled complacently. 'And about thirty-five?' I nodded. 'And not married?' 'No.'

'Well then,' he said, 'you're a damn lucky fellow to be travelling the world with no one to impede you.'

Then he went on to discuss the expenses of travelling.

'You'll likely be paying twenty pounds for this trip,' he said, 'with getting your lodging and buying your tickets, till you're back in the city of Dublin?'

I told him my expenses were not so heavy.

'Maybe you don't drink so,' said his wife, who was near us, 'and that way your living wouldn't be so costly at all.'

An interruption was made by a stop at a small station and the entrance of a ragged ballad-singer, who sang a long ballad about the sorrows of mothers who see all their children going away from them to America.

Further on, when the carriage was much emptier, a middle-aged man got in, and we began discussing the fishing season, Aran fishing, hookers, nobbies and mackerel. I could see, while we were talking, that he, in his turn, was examining me with curiosity. At last he seemed satisfied.

'Begob,' he said, 'I see what you are; you're a fish-dealer.'

It turned out that he was the skipper of a trawler, and we had a long talk, the two of us and a local man who was going to Dingle also.

'There was one time a Frenchman below,' said the skipper, 'who got married here and settled down and worked with the rest of us. One day we were outside in the trawler, and there was a French boat anchored a bit of a way off. "Come on," says Charley — that was his name — "and see can we get some brandy from that boat beyond." "How would we get brandy," says I, "when we've no fish, or meat, or cabbages or a thing at all to offer them?" He went down below then to see what he could get. At that time there were four men only working the trawler, and in the heavy season there were eight. Well, up he comes again and eight plates under his arm. "There are eight plates," says he, "and four will do us; so we'll take out the other four and make a swap with them for brandy." With that he set the eight plates on the deck and began walking up and down and looking on them.

' "The devil mend you," says I. "Will you take them up and come on, if you're coming?"

' "I will," says he, "surely. I'm choicing out the ones that have pictures on them, for it's that kind they do set store on." '

Afterwards we began talking of boats that had been upset during the winter, and lives that had been lost in the neighbourhood.

'A while since,' said the local man, 'there were three men out in a canoe, and the sea rose on them. They tried to come in under the cliff, but they couldn't come to land with the greatness of the waves that were breaking. There were two young men in the canoe, and another man was sixty, or near it. When the young men saw they couldn't bring in the canoe, they said they'd make a jump for the rocks and let her go without them, if she must go. Then they pulled in on the next wave, and when they were close in the two young men jumped on to a rock, but the old man was too stiff, and he was washed back again in the canoe. It came on dark after that, and all thought he was drowned, and they held his wake in Dunquin. At that time there used to be a steamer going in and out trading in Valentia and Dingle and Cahirciveen, and when she came into Dingle, two or three days after, there was my man on board her, as hearty as a salmon. When he was washed back he got one of the oars, and kept her head to the wind; then the tide took him one bit and the wind took him another, and he wrought and he wrought till he was safe beyond in Valentia. Wasn't that a great wonder?' Then as he was ending his story we ran down into Dingle.

Often, when one comes back to a place that one's memory and imagination have been busy with, there is a feeling of smallness and disappointment, and it is a day or two before one can renew all one's enjoyment. This morning, however, when I went up the gap between Croagh Martin and then back to Slea Head, and saw Innishtooskert and Inishvickillaun and the Great Blasket Island itself, they seemed ten times more grey and wild and magnificent than anything I had kept in my memory. The cold sea and surf, and the feeling of winter in the clouds, and the blackness of the rocks, and the red fern everywhere, were a continual surprise and excitement.

Here and there on my way I met old men with tail-coats of frieze, that are becoming so uncommon. When I spoke to them in English they shook their heads and muttered something I could not hear; but when I tried Irish they made me long speeches about the weather and the clearness of the day.

In the evening, as I was coming home, I got a glimpse that seemed to have the whole character of a Corkaguiney — a little line of low cottages with yellow roofs, and an elder tree without leaves beside them, standing out against a high mountain that seemed far away, yet was near enough to be dense and rich and wonderful in its colour.

Then I wandered round the wonderful forts of Fahan. The blueness of the sea and the hills from Carrantuohill to the Skelligs, the singular loneliness of the hillside I was on, with a few choughs and gulls in sight only, had a splendour that was almost a grief in the mind.

34. Cahirciveen

I TURNED into a little public-house this evening, where Maurice — the fisherman I have spoken of before — and some of his friends often sit when it is too wild for fishing. While we were talking a man came in, and joined rather busily in what was being said, though I could see he was not belonging to the place. He moved his position several times till he was quite close to me, then he whispered: 'Will you stand me a medium, mister? I'm hard set for money this while past.' When he had got his medium he began to give me his history. He was a journeyman tailor who had been a year or more in the place, and was beginning to pick up a little Irish to get along with. When he had gone we had a long talk about the making of canoes and the difference between those used in Connaught and Munster.

'They have beein in this country,' said Maurice, 'for twenty or twenty-five years only, and before that we had boats; a canoe will cost twelve pounds, or maybe thirteen pounds, and there is one old man beyond who charges fifteen pounds. If it is well done a canoe will stand for eight years, and you can get a new skin on it when the first one is gone.'

I told him I thought canoes had been in Connemara since the beginning of the world.

'That may well be,' he went on, 'for there was a certain man going out as a pilot, up and down into Clare, and it was he made them first in this place. It is a trade few can learn, for it is all done within the head; you will have to sit down and think it out, and then make up when it is all ready in your mind.'

I described the fixed thole-pins that are used in Connaught — here they use two freely moving thole-pins, with the oar loose between them, and they jeered at the simplicity of the Connaught system. Then we got on the relative value of canoes and boats.

'They are not better than boats,' said Maurice, 'but they are more useful. Before you get a heavy boat swimming you will be wet up to your waist, and then you will be sitting the whole night like that; but a canoe will swim in a handful of water, so that you can get in dry and be dry and warm the whole night. Then there will be seven men in a big boat and seven shares of the fish; but in a canoe there will be three men only and three shares of the fish, though the nets are the same in the two.'

After a while a man sang a song, and then we began talking of tunes and playing the fiddle, and I told them how hard it was to get any sound out of one in a cottage with a floor of earth and a thatched roof over you.

'I can believe that,' said one of the men. 'There was a man a while since went into Tralee to buy a fiddle; and when he went into the shop an old fiddler followed him into it, thinking maybe he'd get the price of a pint. Well, the man was within choicing the fiddles, maybe forty of them, and the old fiddler whispered to him to take them out into the air, "for there's many a fiddle would sound well in here wouldn't be worth a curse outside," says he; so he was bringing them out and bringing them out till he found a good one among them."

This evening, after a day of teeming rain, it cleared for an hour, and I went

35. Blasket Islands

out while the sun was setting to a little cove where a high sea was running. As I was coming back the darkness began to close in except in the west, where there was a red light under the clouds. Against this light I could see patches of open wall and little fields of stooks, and a bit of laneway with an old man driving white cows before him. These seemed transfigured beyond any description.

Then I passed two men riding bare-backed towards the west, who spoke to me in Irish, and a little further on I came to the only village on my way. The ground rose towards it, and as I came near there was a grey bar of smoke from every cottage going up to the low clouds overhead, and standing out strangely against the blackness of the mountain behind the village.

Beyond the patch of wet cottages I had another stretch of lonely roadway, and a heron kept flapping in front of me, rising and lighting again with many lonely cries that made me glad to reach the little public-house near Smerwick.

IN CONNEMARA

FROM GALWAY TO GORUMNA

SOME OF THE worst portions of the Irish congested districts — of which so much that is contradictory has been spoken and written — lie along the further north coast of Galway Bay, and about the whole seaboard from Spiddal to Clifden. Some distance inland there is a line of railway, and in the bay itself a steamer passes in and out to the Aran Islands; but this particular district can only be visited through driving or riding over some thirty or forty miles of desolate roadway. If one takes this route from Galway one has to go a little way only to reach places and people that are fully typical of Connemara. On each side of the road one sees small square fields of oats, or potatoes, or pasture, divided by loose stone walls that are built up without mortar. Wherever there are a few cottages near the road one sees bare-footed women hurrying backwards and forwards, with hampers of turf or grass slung over their backs, and generally a few children running after them, and if it is a market-day, as was the case on the day of which I am going to write, one overtakes long strings of country people driving home from Galway in low carts drawn by an ass or pony. As a rule one or two men sit in front of the cart driving and smoking, with a couple of women behind them stretched out at their ease among sacks of flour or young pigs, and nearly always talking continuously in Gaelic. These men are all dressed in homespuns of the grey natural wool, and the women in deep madder-dyed petticoats and bodices, with brown shawls over their heads. One's first feeling as one comes back among these people and takes a place, so to speak, in this noisy procession of fishermen, farmers, and women, where nearly everyone is interesting and attractive, is a dread of any reform that would tend to lessen their individuality rather than any very real hope of improving their well-being. One feels then, perhaps a little later, that it is part of the misfortune of Ireland that nearly all the characteristics which give colour and attractiveness to Irish life are bound up with a social condition that is near to penury, while in countries like Brittany the best external features of the local life — the rich embroidered dresses, for instance, or the carved furniture — are connected with a decent and comfortable social condition.

About twelve miles from Galway one reaches Spiddal, a village which lies on the borderland between the fairly prosperous districts near Galway and the barren country further to the west. Like most places of its kind, it has a double row of houses — some of them with two storeys — several public-houses with a large police barrack among them, and a little to one side a coastguard station, ending up at either side of the village with a chapel and a church. It was evening when we drove into Spiddal, and a little after sunset we walked on to a rather exposed quay, where a few weather-beaten hookers were moored with many ropes. As we came down none of the crews were to be seen, but threads of turf-smoke rising from the open manhole of the forecastle showed that the men were probably on board. While we were looking down on them from the pier — the tide was far out — an old grey-haired man, with the inflamed eyes that are so common here from the continual itching of the turf-smoke, peered up through the manhole and watched us with vague curiosity. A few moments later a young man came down from a field of black earth, where he had been digging a drain, and asked the old man, in Gaelic, to throw him a spark for his pipe. The latter disappeared for a moment, then came up again with a smouldering end of a turf sod in his hand, and threw it up on the pier, where the young man caught it with a quick downward grab without burning himself, blew it into a blaze, lit his pipe with it, and went back to his work. These people are so poor that many of them do not spend any money on matches. The spark of lighting turf is kept alive day and night on the hearth, and when a man goes out fishing or to work in the fields he usually carries a lighted sod with him, and keeps it all day buried in ashes or any dry rubbish, so that he can use it when he needs it. On our way back to the village an old woman begged from us, speaking in English, as most of the people do to anyone who is not a native. We gave her a few halfpence, and as she was moving away with an ordinary 'God save you!' I said a blessing to her in Irish to show her I knew her own language if she chose to use it. Immediately she turned back towards me and began her thanks again, this time with extraordinary profusion. 'That the blessing of God may be on you,' she said, 'on road and on ridgeway, on sea and on land, on flood and on mountain, in all the kingdoms of the world' — and so on, till I was too far off to hear what she was saying.

In a district like Spiddal one sees curious gradations of type, especially on Sundays and holidays, when everyone is dressed as their fancy leads them and as well as they can manage. As I watched the people coming from Mass the morning after we arrived this was curiously noticeable. The police and coastguards came first in their smartest uniforms; then the shopkeepers, dressed like the people of Dublin, but a little more grotesquely; then the more well-to-do country folk dressed only in the local clothes I have spoken of, but the best and newest kind, while the wearers themselves looked well-fed and healthy, and a few of them, especially the girls, magnificently built; then, last of all, one saw the destitute in still the same clothes, but this time patched and threadbare and ragged, the women mostly barefooted, and both sexes pinched with hunger and the fear of it. The class that one would be most interested to see increase is that of the typical well-to-do people, but except in a few districts it is not numerous, and it is always aspiring after the dress of the shop-people or tending to sink down again among the paupers.

Later in the day we drove on another long stage to the west. As before, the country we passed through was not depressing, though stony and barren as a quarry. At every crossroads we passed groups of young, healthy-looking boys

36. Carraroe

and men amusing themselves with hurley or pitching, and further back on little heights, a small field's breadth from the road, there were many groups of girls sitting out by the hour, near enough to the road to see everything that was passing, yet far enough away to keep their shyness undisturbed. Their red dresses looked peculiarly beautiful among the fresh green of the grass and opening bracken, with a strip of sea behind them, and, far away, the grey cliffs of Clare. A little further on, some ten miles from Spiddal, inlets of the sea begin to run in towards the mountains, and the road turns north to avoid them across an expanse of desolate bog far more dreary than the rocks of the coast. Here one sees a few wretched sheep nibbling in places among the turf, and occasionally a few ragged people walking rapidly by the roadside. Before we stopped for the night we had reached another bay coast-line, and were among stones again. Later in the evening we walked out round another small quay, with the usual little band of shabby hookers, and then along a road that rose in some places a few hundred feet above the sea; and as one looked down into the little fields that lay below it, they looked so small and rocky that the very thought of tillage in them seemed like the freak of an eccentric. Yet in this particular place tiny cottages, some of them without windows, swarmed by the roadside and in the 'boreens,' or laneways, at either side, many of them built on a single sweep of stone with the naked living rock for their floor. A number of people were to be seen everywhere about them, the men loitering by the roadside and the women hurrying among the fields, feeding an odd calf or lamb, or driving in a few ducks before the night. In one place a few boys were playing pitch with trousers buttons, and a little further on half-a-score of young men were making donkeys jump backwards and forwards over a low wall. As we came back we met two men, who came and talked to us, one of them, by his hat and dress, plainly a man who had been away from Connemara. In a little while he told us that he had been in Gloucester and Bristol working on public works, but had wearied of it and come back to his country.

'Bristol,' he said, 'is the greatest town, I think, in all England, but the work in it is hard.'

I asked him about the fishing in the neighbourhood we were in. 'Ah,' he said, 'there's little fishing in it at all, for we have no good boats. There is no one asking for boats for this place, for the shopkeepers would rather have the people idle, so that they can get them for a shilling a day to go out in their old hookers and sell turf in Aran and on the coast of Clare.' Then we talked of Aran, and he told me of people I knew there who had died or got married since I had been on the islands, and then they went on their way.

BETWEEN THE BAYS OF CARRAROE

IN RURAL Ireland very few parishes only are increasing in population, and those that are doing so are usually in districts of the greatest poverty. One of the most curious instances of this tendency is to be found in the parish of Carraroe, which is said to be, on the whole, the poorest parish in the country, although many worse cases of individual destitution can be found elsewhere. The most characteristic part of this district lies on a long promontory between Cashla Bay and Greatman's Bay. On both coast-lines one sees a good many small quays, with, perhaps, two hookers moored to them, and on the roads one passes an occasional flat space covered with small green fields of oats — with whole families on their knees weeding among them — or patches of potatoes; but for the rest one sees little but an endless series of low stony hills, with veins of grass. Here and there, however, one comes in sight of a fresh-water lake, with an island or two, covered with seagulls, and many cottages round the shore; some of them standing almost on the brink of the water, others a little higher up, fitted in among the rocks, and one or two standing out on the top of a ridge against the blue of the sky or of the Twelve Bens of Connaught.

At the edge of one of these lakes, near a school of lace or knitting — one of those that have been established by the Congested Districts Board — we met a man driving a mare and foal that had scrambled out of their enclosure, although the mare had her two off-legs chained together. As soon as he got them back into one of the fields and built up the wall with loose stones, he came over to a stone beside us and began to talk about horses and the dying out of the ponies of Connemara. 'You will hardly get any real Connemara ponies now at all,' he said; 'and the kind of horses they send down to us to improve the breed are no use, for the horses we breed from them will not thrive or get their health on the little patches where we have to put them. This last while most of the people in this parish are giving up horses altogether. Those that have them sell their foals when they are about six months old for four pounds, or five maybe; but the better part of the people are working with an ass only, that can carry a few things on a straddle over her back.'

'If you've got no horses,' I said, 'how do you get to Galway if you want to go to a fair or to market?'

'We go by the sea,' he said, 'in one of the hookers you've likely seen at the little quays while walking down by the road. You can sail to Galway if the wind is fair in four hours or less maybe; and the people here are all used to the sea, for no one can live in this place but by cutting turf in the mountains and sailing out to sell it in Clare or Aran, for you see yourselves there's no good in the land, that has little in it but bare rocks and stones. Two years ago there came a wet summer, and the people were worse off then than they are now maybe, with their bad potatoes and all; for they couldn't cut or dry a load of turf to sell across the bay, and there was many a woman hadn't a dry sod itself to put under her pot, and she shivering with cold and hunger.'

A little later, when we had talked of one or two other things, I asked him if many of the people who were living round in the scattered cottages we could see were often in real want of food. 'There are a few, maybe, have enough at all times,' he said, 'but the most are in want one time or another, when the potatoes are bad or few, and their whole store is eaten; and there are some who are near starving all times, like a widow woman beyond who has seven children with hardly a shirt on their skins, and they with nothing to eat but the milk from one cow, and a handful of meal they will get from one neighbour or another.'

'You're getting an old man,' I said, 'and do you remember if the place was as

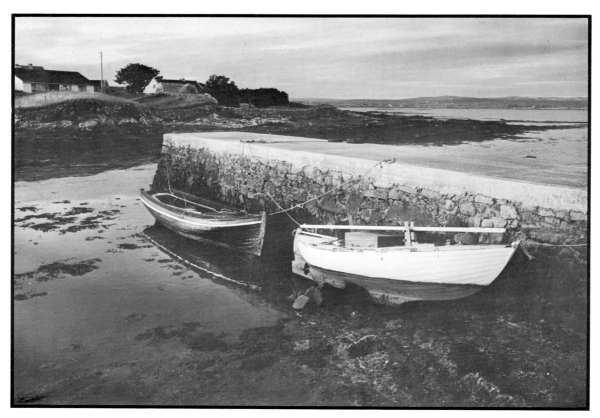

37. Near Costelloe

bad as it is now when you were a young man growing up?'

'It wasn't as bad, or a half as bad,' he said, 'for there were fewer people in it and more land to each, and the land itself was better at the time, for now it is drying up or something, and not giving its fruits and increase as it did.'

I asked him if they used bought manures.

'We get a hundredweight for eight shillings now and again, but I think there's little good in it, for it's only a poor kind they send out to the like of us. Then there was another thing they had in the old times,' he continued, 'and that was the making of poteen (illicit whisky), for it was a great trade at that time, and you'd see the police down on their knees blowing the fire with their own breath to make a drink for themselves, and then going off with the butt of an old barrel, and that was one seizure, and an old bag with a handful of malt, and that was another seizure, and would satisfy the law; but now they must have the worm and the still and a prisoner, and there is little of it made in the country. At that time a man would get ten shillings for a gallon, and it was a good trade for poor people.'

As we were talking a woman passed driving two young pigs, and we began to speak of them.

'We buy the young pigs and rear them up,' he said, 'but this year they are scarce and dear. And indeed what good are they in bad years, for how can we go feeding a pig when we haven't enough, maybe, for ourselves? In good years, when you have potatoes and plenty, you can rear up two or three pigs and make a good bit on them; but other times, maybe, a poor man will give a pound for a young pig that won't thrive after, and then his pound will be gone, and he'll have no money for his rent.'

The old man himself was cheerful and seemingly fairly well-to-do; but in the end he seemed to be getting dejected as he spoke of one difficulty after another, so I asked him, to change the subject, if there was much dancing in the country. 'No,' he said, 'this while back you'll never see a piper coming this way at all, though in the old times it's many a piper would be moving around through those houses for a whole quarter together, playing his pipes and drinking poteen and the people dancing round him; but now there is no dancing or singing in this place at all, and most of the young people is growing up and going to America.'

I pointed to the lace-school near us, and asked how the girls got on with the lace, and if they earned much money. 'I've heard tell,' he said, 'that in the four schools round about this place there is near six hundred pounds paid out in wages every year, and that is a good sum; but there isn't a young girl going to them that isn't saving up, and saving up till she'll have enough gathered to take her to America, and then away she will go, and why wouldn't she?'

Often the worst moments in the lives of these people are caused by the still frequent outbreaks of typhus fever, and before we parted I asked him if there was much fever in the particular district where we were.

'Just here,' he said, 'there isn't much of it at all, but there are places round about where you'll sometimes hear of a score and more stretched out waiting for their death; but I suppose it is the will of God. Then there is a sickness they call consumption that some will die of; but I suppose there is no place where people aren't getting their death one way or other, and the most in this place are enjoying good health, glory be to God! for it is a healthy place and there is a clean air blowing.'

Then, with a few of the usual blessings, he got up and left us, and we walked on through more of similar or still poorer country. It is remarkable that from Spiddal onward — that is, in the whole of the most poverty-stricken district in Ireland — no one begs, even in a roundabout way. It is the fashion, with many of the officials who are connected with relief works and such things, to compare the people of this district rather unfavourably with the people of the poor districts of Donegal; but in this respect at least Donegal is not the more admirable.

AMONG THE RELIEF WORKS

BEYOND CARRAROE, the last promontory on the north coast of Galway Bay, one reaches a group of islands which form the lower angle of Connemara. These islands are little more than a long peninsula broken through by a number of small straits, over which, some twelve years ago, causeways and swing-bridges were constructed, so that one can now drive straight on through Annaghvaan, Lettermore, Gorumna, Lettermullan, and one or two smaller islands. When one approaches this district from the east a long detour is made to get round the inner point of Greatman's Bay, and then the road turns to the south-west till one reaches Annaghvaan, the first of the islands. This road is a remarkable one. Nearly every foot of it, as it now stands, has been built up in different years of famine by the people of the neighbourhood working on Government relief works, which are now once more in full swing; making improvements in some places, turning primitive tracts into roadways in others, and here and there building a new route to some desolate village.

We drove many miles, with Costello and Carraroe behind us, along a bog-road of curious formation built up on a turf embankment, with broad grassy sods at either side — perhaps to make a possible way for the barefooted people — then two spaces of rough broken stones where the wheel-ruts are usually worn, and in the centre a track of gritty earth for the horses. Then, at a turn of the road, we came in sight of a dozen or more men and women working hurriedly and doggedly improving a further portion of this road, with a ganger swaggering among them and directing their work. Some of the people were cutting out sods from grassy patches near the road, others were carrying down bags of earth in a slow, inert procession, a few were breaking stones, and three or four women were scraping out a sort of sandpit at a little distance. As we drove quickly by we could see that every man and woman was working with a sort of hang-dog dejection that would be enough to make any casual passer mistake them for a band of convicts. The wages given on these works are usually a shilling a day, and, as a rule, one person only, generally the head of the family, is taken from each house. Sometimes the best worker in a family is thus forced away from his ordinary work of farming, or fishing, or kelp-making for this wretched remuneration at a time when his private industry is most needed. If this system of relief has some things in its favour, it is far from

38. Turf-cutting, southwest Galway

satisfactory in other ways, and is not always economical. I have been told of a district not very far from here where there is a ganger, an overseer, an inspector, a paymaster, and an engineer superintending the work of two paupers only. This is possibly an exaggerated account of what is really taking place, yet it probably shows, not too inexactly, a state of things that is not rare in Ireland.

A mile or two further on we passed a similar band of workers, and then the road rose for a few feet and turned sharply on to a long causeway, with a swing-bridge in the centre, that led to the island of Annaghvaan. Just as we reached the bridge our driver jumped down and took his mare by the head. A moment later she began to take fright at the hollow noise of her own hoofs on the boards of the bridge and the blue rush of the tide which she could see through them, but the man coaxed her forward, and got her over without much difficulty. For the next mile or two there was a continual series of small islands and causeways and bridges that the mare grew accustomed to, and trotted gaily over, till we reached Lettermore, and drove for some distance through the usual small hills of stone. Then we came to the largest causeway of all, between Lettermore and Gorumna, where the proportion of the opening of the bridge to the length of the embankment is so small that the tide runs through with extraordinary force. On the outer side the water was banked up nearly a yard high against the buttress of the bridge, and on the other side there was a rushing, eddying torrent that recalled some mountain salmon-stream in flood, except that here, instead of the brown river-water, one saw the white and blue foam of the sea.

The remainder of our road to the lower western end of Gorumna led through hilly districts that became more and more white with stone, though one saw here and there a few brown masses of bog or an oblong lake with many islands and rocks. In most places, if one looked round the hills a little distance from the road, one could see the yellow roofs and white gables of cottages scattered everywhere through this waste of rock; and on the ridge of every hill one could see the red dresses of women who were gathering turf or looking for their sheep or calves. Near the village where we stopped things are somewhat better, and a few fields of grass and potatoes were to be seen, and a certain number of small cattle grazing among the rocks. Here also one is close to the sea, and fishing and kelp-making are again possible. In the village there is a small private quay in connection with a shop where everything is sold, and not long after we arrived a hooker sailed in with a cargo of supplies from Galway. A number of women were standing about expecting her arrival, and soon afterwards several of them set off for different parts of the island with a bag of flour slung over an ass. One of these, a young girl of seventeen or eighteen, drove on with her load far into Lettermullan, the next island, on a road that we were walking also; and then sent the ass back to Gorumna in charge of a small boy, and took up the sack of flour, which weighed at least sixteen stone, on her back, and carried it more than a mile, through a narrow track, to her own home. This practice of allowing young girls to carry great weights frequently injures them severely, and is the cause of much danger and suffering in their after lives. They do not seem, however, to know anything of the risks they run, and their loads are borne gaily.

A little further on we came on another stretch of the relief works, where there were many elderly men and young girls working with the same curious aspect of shame and dejection. The work was just closing for the evening, and as we walked back to Gorumna an old man who had been working walked with us, and complained of his great poverty and the small wages he was given. 'A shilling a day,' he said, 'would hardly keep a man in tea and sugar and tobacco and a bit of bread to eat, and what good is it at all when there is a family of five or six maybe, and often more?' Just as we reached the swing-bridge that led back to Gorumna, another hooker sailed carefully in through the narrow rocky channel, with a crowd of men and women sitting along the gunwale. They edged in close to a flat rock near the bridge, and made her fast for a moment while the women jumped on shore; some of them carrying bottles, others with little children, and all dressed out in new red petticoats and shawls. They looked as they crowded up on the road as fine a body of peasant women as one could see anywhere, and were all talking and laughing eagerly among themselves. The old man told me in Irish that they had been at a pattern — a sort of semi-religious festival like the well-known festivals of Brittany — that had just been held some distance to the east on the Galway coast. It was reassuring to see that some, at least, of these island people are, in their own way, prosperous and happy. When the women were all landed the swing-bridge was pushed open, and the hooker was poled through to the bay on the north side of the islands. Then the men moored her and came up to a little public-house, where they spent the rest of the evening talking and drinking and telling stories in Irish.

THE FERRYMAN OF DINISH ISLAND

WHEN WANDERING among lonely islands in the west of Ireland, like those of the Gorumna group, one seldom fails to meet with some old sailor or pilot who has seen something of the world, and it is often from a man of this kind that one learns more about the island or hill that he has come back to, in middle age or towards the end of his life. An old seafaring man who ferries chance comers to and from Dinish Island is a good example of this class. The island is separated from Furnace — the last of the group that is linked together by causeways and bridges — by a deep channel between two chains of rock. As we went to this channel across a strip of sandhill a wild-looking old man appeared at the other side, and began making signs to us and pushing off a heavy boat from the shore. Before he was half-way across we could hear him calling out to us in a state of almost incoherent excitement, and directing us to a ledge of rock where he could take us off. A moment later we scrambled into his boat upon a mass of seaweed that he had been collecting for kelp, and he poled us across, talking at random about how he had seen His Royal Highness the Duke of Edinburgh, and gone to America as interpreter for the emigrants in a bad season twenty-one years ago. As soon as we landed we walked across a bay of sand to a tiny schoolhouse close to the sea, and the old man turned back across the channel with a travelling tea merchant and a young girl who had come down to the shore. All the time they were going across we could hear him talking and vociferating at the top of his voice, and then, after a moment's

39. *Religious Statues, Ballinrobe*

silence, he came in sight again, on our side, running towards us over the sand. After he had been a little while with us, and got over the excitement caused by the sudden arrival of two strangers — we could judge how great it was by a line of children's heads who were peeping over the rocks and watching us with amazement — he began to talk clearly and simply. After a few of the remarks one hears from everyone about the loneliness of the place, he spoke about the school behind us.

'Isn't is a poor thing,' he said, 'to see a school lying closed up the like of that, and twenty or thirty scholars, maybe, running wild along the sea? I am very lonesome since that school was closed, for there was a schoolmistress used to come for a long while from Lettermullan, and I used to ferry her over the water, and maybe ten little children along with her. And then there was a mistress living here for a while, and I used to ferry the children only; but now she has found herself a better place, and this three months there's no school in it at all.'

One could see when he was quiet that he differed a good deal, both in face and in his way of speaking, from the people of the islands, and when he paused I asked him if he had spent all his life among them, excepting the one voyage to America.

'I have not,' he said; 'but I've been in many places, though I and my fathers have rented the sixth of this island for near two hundred years. My own father was a sailor-man who came in here by chance and married a woman, and lived, a snug, decent man, with five cows or six, till he died at a hundred and three. And my mother's father, who had the place before him, died at a hundred and eight, and he wouldn't have died then, I'm thinking, only he fell down and broke his hip. They were strong, decent people at that time, and I was going to school — travelling out over the islands with my father ferrying me — till I was twenty years of age; and then I went to America and got to be a sailorman, and was in New York, and Baltimore, and New Orleans, and after that I was coasting till I knew every port and town of this country and Scotland and Wales.'

One of us asked him if he had stayed at sea till he came back to this island.

'I did not,' he said, 'for I went ashore once in South Wales, and I'm telling you Wales is a long country, for I travelled all a whole summer's day from that place till I reached Birkenhead at nine o'clock. And then I went to Manchester and to Newcastle-on-Tyne, and I worked there for two years. That's a rich country, dear gentlemen, and when the paymen would come into the works on a Saturday you'd see the bit of board he had over his shoulder bending down with the weight of sovereigns he had for the men. And isn't it a queer thing to be sitting here now thinking on those times, and I after being near twenty years back on this bit of a rock that a dog wouldn't look at, where the pigs die and the spuds die, and even the judges and quality do come out and do lower our rents when they see the wild Atlantic driving in across the cursed stones.'

'And what is it brought you back,' I said, 'if you were doing well beyond in the world?'

'My two brothers went to America,' he said, 'and I had to come back because I was the eldest son, and I got married then, and I after holding out till I was forty. I have a young family now growing up, for I was snug for a while; and then bad times came, and I lost my wife, and the potatoes went bad, and three cows I had were taken in the night with some disease of the brain, and they swam out and were drowned in the sea. I got back their bodies in the morning, and took them down to a gentleman beyond who understands the diseases of animals, but he gave me nothing for them at all. So there I am now with no pigs, and no cows, and a young family running round with no mother to mind them; and what can you do with children that know nothing at all, and will often put down as much in the pot one day as would do three days, and do be wasting the meal, though you can't say a word against them, for it's young and ignorant they are? If it wasn't for them I'd be off this evening, and I'd earn my living easy on the sea, for I'm only fifty-seven years of age, and I have good health; but how can I leave my young children? And I don't know what way I'm to go on living in this place that the Lord created last, I'm thinking, in the end of time; and it's often when I sit down and look around on it I do begin cursing and damning, and asking myself how poor people can go on executing their religion at all.'

For a while he said nothing, and we could see tears in his eyes; then I asked him how he was living now from one day to another.

'They're letting me out advanced meal and flour from the shop,' he said, 'and I'm to pay it back when I burn a ton of kelp in the summer. For two months I was working on the relief works at a shilling a day, but what good is that for a family? So I've stopped now to rake up weed for a ton, or maybe two tons, of kelp. When I left the works I got my boy put on in my place, but the ganger put him back; and then I got him on again, and the ganger put him back. Then I bought a bottle of ink and a pen and a bit of paper to write a letter and make my complaint, but I never wrote it to this day, for what good is it harming him more than another? Then I've a daughter in America has only been there nine months, and she's sent me three pounds already. I have another daughter, living above with her married sister, will be ready to go in autumn, and another little one will go when she's big enough. There is a man above has four daughters in America, and gets a pound a quarter from each one of them, and that is a great thing for a poor man. It's to America we'll all be going, and isn't it a fearful thing to think I'll be kept here another ten years, maybe, tending the children and striving to keep them alive, when I might be abroad in America living in decency and earning my bread?'

Afterwards he took us up to the highest point of the island, and showed us a fine view of the whole group and of the Atlantic beyond them, with a few fishing-boats in the distance, and many large boats nearer the rocks rowing heavily with loads of weed. When we got into the ferry again the channel had become too deep to pole, and the old man rowed with a couple of long sweeps from the bow.

'I go out alone in this boat,' he said, as he was rowing, 'across the bay to the northern land. There is no other man in the place that would do it, but I'm a licensed pilot these twenty years, and a seafaring man.'

Then as we finally left him he called after us:

'It has been a great consolation to me, dear gentlemen, to be talking with your like, for one sees few people in this place, and so may God bless and reward you and see you safely to your homes.'

40. *Mullet Peninsula*

41. Fisherman and Lobster Pots, Slash, Blacksod Bay

THE KELP MAKERS

SOME OF those who have undertaken to reform the congested districts have shown an unfortunate tendency to give great attention to a few canonised industries, such as horse-breeding and fishing, or even bee-keeping, while they neglect local industries that have been practised with success for a great number of years. Thus,
in the large volume issued a couple of years ago by the Department of Agriculture and Technical Instruction for Ireland, which claims to give a comprehensive account of the economic resources of the country, hardly a word has been said of the kelp industry, which is a matter of the greatest importance to the inhabitants of a very large district. The Congested Districts Board seems to have left it on one side also, and in the Galway neighbourhood, at least, no steps appear to have been taken to ensure the people a fair market for the kelp they produce, or to revise the present unsatisfactory system by which it is tested and paid for. In some places the whole buying trade falls into the hands of one man, who can then control the prices at his pleasure, while one hears on all sides of arbitrary decisions by which good kelp is rejected, and what the people consider an inferior article is paid for at a high figure. When the buying is thus carried on no appeal can be made from the decision of one individual, and I have sometimes seen a party of old men sitting nearly in tears on a ton of rejected kelp that had cost them weeks of hard work, while, for all one knew, it had very possibly been refused on account of some grudge or caprice of the buyer.

The village of Trawbaun, which lies on the coast opposite the Aran Islands, is a good instance of a kelp-making neighbourhood. We reached it through a narrow road, now in the hands of the relief workers, where we hurried past the usual melancholy line of old men breaking stones and younger men carrying bags of earth and sods. Soon afterwards the road fell away quickly towards the sea, through a village of many cottages huddled together, with bare walls of stone that had never been whitewashed, as often happens in places that are peculiarly poor. Passing through these, we came out on three or four acres of sandhill that brought us to a line of rocks with a narrow sandy cove between them just filling with the tide. All along the coast, a little above high-water mark, we could see a number of tall, reddish stacks of dried seaweed, some of which had probably been standing for weeks, while others were in various unfinished stages, or had only just been begun. A number of men and women and boys were hard at work in every direction, gathering fresh weed and spreading it out to dry on the rocks. In some places the weed is mostly gathered from the foreshore; but in this neighbourhood, at least in the early summer, it is pulled up from rocks under the sea at low water, by men working from a boat or curagh with a long pole furnished with a short crossbar nailed to the top, which they entangle in the weeds. Just as we came down a curagh, lightly loaded by two boys, was coming in over a low bar into the cove I have spoken of, and both of them were slipping over the side every moment or two to push their canoe from behind. Several bare-legged girls, crooning merry songs in Gaelic, were passing backwards and forwards over the sand, carrying heavy loads of weed on their backs. Further out many other curaghs, more heavily laden, were coming slowly in, waiting for the tide; and some old men on the shore were calling out directions to their crews in the high-pitched tone that is so remarkable in this Connaught Irish. The whole scene, with the fresh smell of the sea and the blueness of the shallow waves, made a curious contrast with the dismal spectacle of the relief workers we had just passed, for here the people seemed as light-hearted as a party of schoolboys.

Further on we came to a rocky headland where some men were burning down their weed into kelp, a process that in this place is given nearly twelve hours. As we came up dense volumes of rich, creamy-coloured smoke were rising from a long pile of weed, in the centre of which we could see here and there a molten mass burning at an intense heat. Two men and a number of boys were attending to the fire, laying on fresh weed wherever the covering grew thin enough to receive it. A little to one side a baby, rolled up in a man's coat, was asleep beside a hamper, as on occasions like this the house is usually shut up and the whole family scatters for work of various kinds. The amount of weed needed to make a ton of kelp varies, I have been told, from three tons to five. The men of a family working busily on a favourable day can take a ton of the raw weed, and the kelp is sold at from three pounds fifteen shillings or a little less to five pounds a ton, so it is easy to see the importance of this trade. When all the weed intended for one furnace has been used the whole is covered up and left three or four days to cool; then it is broken up and taken off in boats or curaghs to a buyer. He takes a handful, tests it with certain chemicals, and fixes the price accordingly; but the people themselves have no means of knowing whether they are getting fair play, and although many buyers may be careful and conscientious, there is a very general feeling of dissatisfaction among the people with the way they are forced to carry on the trade. When the kelp has been finally disposed of it is shipped in schooners and sent away — for the most part, I believe, to Scotland, where it is used for the manufacture of iodine.

Complaints are often heard about the idleness of the natives of Connemara; yet at the present time one sees numbers of the people drying and arranging their weed until nightfall, and the bays where the weed is found are filled with boats at four or five o'clock in the morning, when the tide is favourable. The chances of a good kelp season depend, to some extent, on suitable weather for drying and burning the weed; yet on the whole this trade is probably less precarious than the fishing industry or any other source of income now open to the people of a large portion of these congested districts. In the present year the weather has been excellent, and there is every hope that a good quantity of kelp may be obtained. The matter is of peculiar importance this year, as for the last few months the shop-keepers have been practically keeping the people alive by giving out meal and flour on the security of the kelp harvest — one house alone, I am told, distributed fourteen tons during the last ten days — so that if the kelp should not turn out well, or the prices should be less than what is expected, whole districts will be placed in the greatest difficulty.

It is a remarkable feature of the domestic finance of this district that, although the people are so poor, they are used to dealing with fairly large sums of money. Thus four or five tons of kelp well sold may bring a family between twenty and thirty pounds, and their bills for flour (which is bought in bags of two hundred-weight at a good deal over a pound a bag) must also be considerable. It is the same with their pig-farming, fishing, and other industries, and probably this familiarity with considerable sums causes a part, at least, of the sense of shame that is shown by those who are reduced to working on the roadside the miserable pittance of a shilling a day.

THE BOAT BUILDERS

WE LEFT Gorumna in a hooker managed by two men, and sailed north to another district of the Galway coast. Soon after we started the wind fell, and we lay almost becalmed in a curious bay so filled with islands that one could hardly distinguish the channel that led to the open sea. For some time we drifted slowly between Dinish Island and Illaunerach, a stony mound inhabited by three families only. Then our pace became so slow that the boatmen got out a couple of long sweeps and began rowing heavily, with sweat streaming from them. The air was heavy with thunder, and on every side one saw the same smoky blue sea and sky, with grey islands and mountains beyond them, and in one place a ridge of yellow rocks touched by a single ray of sunlight. Two or three pookawns — lateen-rigged boats, said to be of Spanish origin — could be seen about a mile ahead of us sailing easily across our bows, where some opening in the islands made a draught from the east. In half an hour our own sails filled, and the boatmen stopped rowing and began to talk to us. One of them gave us many particulars about the prices of hookers and their nets, and the system adopted by the local boat-builders who work for the poorer fishermen of the neighbourhood.

'When a man wants a boat,' he said, 'he buys the timber from a man in Galway and gets it brought up here in a hooker. Then he gets a carpenter to come to his house and built it in some place convenient to the sea. The whole time the carpenter will be working at it the other man must support him, and give him whisky every day. Then he must stand around while he is working, holding boards and handing nails, and if he doesn't do it smart enough you'll hear the carpenter scolding him and making a row. A carpenter like that will be six weeks or two months, maybe, building a boat, and he will get two pounds for his work when he is done. The wood and everything you need for a fifteen-foot boat will cost four pounds, or beyond it, so a boat like that is a dear thing for a poor man.'

We asked him about the boats that had been made by the local boatwrights for the Congested Districts Board.

'There were some made in Lettermullan,' he said, 'and beyond it an island west of where you're going to-day there is an old man has been building boats for thirty years, and he could tell you all about them.'

Meanwhile we had been sailing quickly, and were near the north shore of the bay. The tide had gone so far out when we were becalmed that it was not possible to get in alongside the pier, so the men steered for a ledge of rock further out, where it was possible to land. As we were going in an anchor was dropped, and then when we were close to the rocks the men checked the boat by straining on the rope, and brought us in to the shore with a great deal of nicety.

42. Lettermullen Island

Not long afterwards we made our way to see the old carpenter the boatmen had told us of, and found him busy with two or three other men caulking the bottom of a boat that was propped up on one side. As we came towards them along the low island shore the scene reminded one curiously of some old picture of Noah building the Ark. The old man himself was rather remarkable in appearance, with strongly formed features, and an extraordinarily hairy chest showing through the open neck of his shirt. He told us that he had made several nobbies for the Board, and showed us an arrangement that had been supplied for steaming the heavy timber needed for boats of this class.

'At the present time,' he said, 'I am making our own boats again, and the fifteen-foot boats the people do use here have light timber, and we don't need to trouble steaming them at all. I get eight pounds for a boat when I buy the timber myself, and fit her all out ready for the sea. But I am working for poor men, and it is often three years before I will be paid the full price of a boat I'm after making.'

From where we stood we could see another island across a narrow sound, studded with the new cottages that are built in this neighbourhood by the Congested Districts Board.

'That island, like another you're after passing, has been bought by the Board,' said the old man, who saw us looking at them; 'and it is a great thing for the poor people to have their holdings arranged for them in one strip instead of the little scattered plots the people have in all this neighbourhood, where a man will often have to pass through the ground of maybe three men to get to a plot of his own.'

This rearrangement of the holdings that is being carried out in most places where estates have been bought up by the Board, and resold to the tenants, is a matter of great importance that is fully appreciated by the people. Mere tenant purchase in districts like this may do some good for the moment by lowering rents and interesting the people in their land; yet in the end it is likely to prove disastrous, as it tends to perpetuate holdings that are not large enough to support their owners and are too scattered to be worked effectively. In the relatively few estates bought by the Board — up to March, 1904, their area amounted to two or three hundred thousand acres out of the three and a half million that are included in the congested districts — this is being set right, yet some of the improvements made at the same time are perhaps a less certain gain, and give the neighbourhoods where they have been made an uncomfortable look that is, I think, felt by the people. For instance, there is no pressing need to substitute iron roofs — in many ways open to objection — for the thatch that has been used for centuries, and is part of the constructive tradition of the people. In many districts the thatching is done in some idle season by the men of a household themselves, with the help of their friends, who are proud of their skill; and it is looked on as a sort of festival where there is great talk and discussion, the loss of which is hardly made up for by the patch of ground which was needed to grow the straw, and is now free for other uses. In the same way, the improvements in the houses built by the Board are perhaps a little too sudden. It is far better, wherever possible, to improve the ordinary prosperity of the people till they begin to improve their houses themselves on their own lines, than to do too much in the way of building houses that have no interest for the people and disfigure the country. I remember one evening, in another congested district — on the west coast of Kerry — listening to some peasants who discussed for hours the proportions of a new cottage that was to be built by one of them. They had never, of course, heard of proportion; but they had rules and opinions, in which they were deeply interested, as to how high a house should be if it was a certain length, with so many rafters, in order that it might look well. Traditions of this kind are destroyed for ever when too sweeping improvements are made in a district, and the loss is a great one. If any real improvement is to be made in many of these congested districts the rearrangement and sale of the holdings to the tenants, somewhat on the lines adopted by the Board, must be carried out on a large scale; but in doing so care should be taken to disorganise as little as possible the life and methods of the people. A little attention to the wells, and, where necessary, greater assistance in putting up sheds for the cattle and pigs that now live in the houses, would do a great deal to get rid of the epidemics of typhus and typhoid, and then the people should be left as free as possible to arrange their houses and way of life as it pleases them.

THE HOMES OF THE HARVESTMEN

THE GENERAL appearance of the North Mayo country round Belmullet — another district of the greatest poverty — differs curiously from that of Connemara. In Mayo a waste of turf and bog takes the place of the waste of stones that is the chief feature of the coast of Galway. Consequently sods of turf are used for all sorts of work — building walls and ditches, and even the gables of cottages — instead of the loose pieces of granite or limestone that are ready to one's hand in the district we have left. Between every field one sees a thin bank of turf, worn away in some places by the weather, and covered in others with loose grass and royal flowering ferns. The rainfall of Belmullet is a heavy one, and in wet weather this absence of stone gives one an almost intolerable feeling of dampness and discomfort.

The last forty miles of our journey to Belmullet was made on the long car which leaves Ballina at four o'clock in the morning. It was raining heavily as we set out, and the whole town was asleep; but during the first hour we met many harvestmen with scythe-handles and little bundles tied in red handkerchiefs, walking quickly into Ballina to embark for Liverpool or Glasgow. Then we passed Crossmolina, and were soon out on the bogs, where one drives for mile after mile, seeing an odd house only, scattered in a few places with long distances between them. We had been travelling all night from Connemara, and again and again we dosed off into a sort of dream, only to wake up with a start when the car gave a dangerous lurch, and see the same dreary waste with a few wet cattle straggling about the road, or the corner of a lake just seen beyond them through a break in the clouds. When we had driven about fifteen miles we changed horses at a village of three houses, where an old man without teeth brought out the new horses and harnessed them slowly, as if he was half in his sleep. Then we drove on again, stopping from time to time at some sort of post-office, where a woman or boy usually came out to take the bag of letters. At Bangor Erris four more passengers got up, and as the roads were heavy with the rain we settled into a slow jog-trot that made us almost despair of arriving at our destination. The people were now at work weeding potatoes in their few patches of tillage, and cutting turf in the bogs, and their draggled, colour-less clothes — so unlike the homespuns of Connemara — added indescribably to the feeling of wretchedness one gets from the sight of these miserable cottages, many of them with an old hamper or the end of a barrel stuck through the roof for a chimney, and the desolation of the bogs.

Belmullet itself is curiously placed on an isthmus — recently pierced by a canal — that divides Broad Haven from Blacksod Bay. Beyond the isthmus there is a long peninsula some fourteen miles in length, running north and south, and separating these two bays from the Atlantic. As we were wandering through this headland in the late afternoon the rain began again, and we stopped to shelter under the gable of a cottage. After a moment or two a girl came out and brought us in out of the rain. At first we could hardly see anything with the darkness of the rain outside the small window and door of the cottage, but after a moment or two we grew accustomed to it, and the light seemed adequate enough. The woman of the house was sitting opposite us at the corner of the fire, with two children near her, and just behind them a large wooden bed with a sort of red covering, and red curtains above it. Then there was the door, and a spinning-wheel, and at the end opposite the fire a couple of stalls for cattle and a place for a pig with an old brood sow in it, and one young one a few weeks old. At the edge of the fireplace a small door opened into an inner room, but in many cottages of this kind there is one apartment only. We talked, as usual, of the hardships of the people, which are worst in places like this, at some distance from the sea, where no help can be got from fishing or making kelp.

'All this land about here,' said the woman, who was sitting by the fire, 'is stripped bog' — that is, bog from which the turf has been cut — 'and it is no use at all without all kinds of stuff and manure mixed through it. If you went down a little behind the house you'd see that there is nothing but stones left at the bottom, and you'd want great quantities of sand and seaweed and dung to make it soft and kind enough to grow a thing in it at all. The big farmers have all the good land snapped up, and there is nothing left but stones and bog for poor people like ourselves.'

The sow was snorting in the corner, and I said, after a moment, that it was probably with the pigs that they made the most of their money.

'In bad years,' she said, 'like the year we've had, when the potatoes are rotten and few, there is no use in our pigs, for we have nothing to give them. Last year we had a litter of pigs from that sow, and they were little good to us, for the people were afraid to buy at any price for fear they'd die upon their hands.'

One of us said something of the relief work we had seen in Connemara.

'We have the same thing here,' she said, 'and I have a young lad who is out working on them now, and he has a little horse beast along with him, so that he gets a week's pay for three days or four, and has a little moment over for our own work on the farm.'

I asked her if she had many head of cattle.

'I have not, indeed,' she said, 'nor any place to feed. There is some small

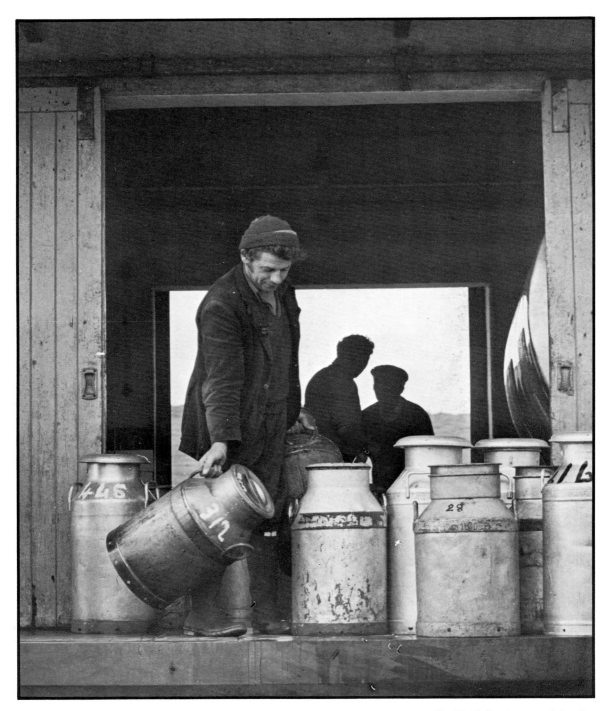

43. Weigh Station, near Belmullet

people do put a couple of yearlings out on the grass you see below you running out to the sands; but where would I get money to buy one, or to pay the one pound eight, or near it, you do pay for every yearling you have upon the grass? A while since,' she went on, 'we weren't so bad as we are at this time, for we had a young lad who used to go to Scotland for the harvest, and be sending us back a pound or two pounds maybe in the month, and bringing five or six or beyond it when he'd come home at the end of autumn; but he got a hurt and never overed it, so we have no one at this time can go from us at all.'

One of the girls had been carding wool for the spinning-wheel, so I asked about the spinning and weaving.

'Most women spin their wool in this place,' she said, 'and the weaver weaves it afterwards for threepence a yard if it is a single weaving, and for sixpence a yard if it is double woven, as we do have it for the men. The women in this place have little time to be spinning, but the women back on the mountains do be mixing colours through their wool till you'd never ask to take your eyes from it. They do be throwing in a bit of stone colour, and a bit of red madder, and a bit of crimson, and a bit of stone colour again, and, believe me, it is nice stuffs they do make that you'd never ask to take your eyes from.'

The shower had now blown off, so we went out again and made our way down to a cover of the sea where a seal was diving at some distance from the shore, putting up its head every few moments to look at us with a curiously human expression. Afterwards we went on to a jetty north of the town, where the Sligo boat had just come in. One of the men told us that they were taking over a hundred harvestmen to Sligo the next morning, where they would take a boat for Glasgow, and that many more would be going during the week. This migratory labour has many unsatisfactory features; yet in the present state of the country it may tend to check the longing for America that comes over those that spend the whole year on one miserable farm.

THE SMALLER PEASANT PROPRIETORS

THE "CAR-DRIVERS" that take one round to isolated places in Ireland seem to be the cause of many of the misleading views that chance visitors take up about the country and the real temperament of the people. These men spend a great deal of their time driving a host of inspectors and officials connected with various Government Boards, who, although they often do excellent work, belong for the most part to classes that have a traditional misconception of the country people. It follows naturally enough that the carmen pick up the views of their patrons, and when they have done so they soon find apt instances from their own local knowledge that give a native popular air to opinions that are essentially foreign. That is not all. The car-driver is usually the only countryman with whom the official is kept in close personal contact; so that, while the stranger is bewildered, many distinguished authorities have been pleased and instructed by this version of their own convictions. It is fair to add that the carman is usually a small-town's man, so that he has a not unnatural grudge against the mountain-squatter, for whom so much has apparently been done, while the towns are neglected, and also that the carman may be generally relied on when he is merely stating facts to anyone who is not a total stranger to the country.

We drove out recently with a man of this class, and as we left Belmullet he began to talk of an estate that has been sold to the tenants by the Congested Districts Board.

'Those people pay one or two pounds in the year,' he said, 'and for that they have a house, and a stripe of tilled land, and a stripe of rough land and an outlet on the mountain for grazing cattle, and the rights of turbary, and yet they aren't satisfied; while I do pay five pounds for a little house with hardly enough land to grow two score of cabbages.'

He was an elderly man, and as we drove on through many gangs of relief workers he told us about the building of the Belmullet Workhouse in 1857, and I asked him what he remembered or had heard of the great famine ten years earlier.

'I have heard my father say,' he said, 'that he often seen the people dragging themselves along to the workhouse in Binghamstown, and some of them falling down and dying on the edge of the road. There were other places where he'd seen four or five corpses piled up on each other against a bit of a bank or the butt of a bridge, and when I began driving I was in great dread in the evenings when I'd be passing those places on the roads.'

It was a dark, windy day, and we went on through endless wastes of brown mountain and bog, meeting no one but an occasional woman driving an ass with meal or flour, or a few people drying turf and building it up into ricks on the roadside or near it. In the distance one could see white roads — often relief roads — twisting among the hills, with no one on them but a man here and there riding in with the mails from some forlorn village. In places we could see the white walls and gables of one of these villages against the face of a hill, and fairly frequently we passed a few tumbled-down cottages with plots of potatoes about them. After a while the carman stopped at a door to get a drink for his horse, and we went in for a moment or two to shelter from the wind. It was the poorest cottage we had seen. There was no chimney, and the smoke rose by the wall to a hole in the roof at the top of the gable. A boy of ten was sitting near the fire minding three babies, and at the other end of the room there was a cow with two calves and a few sickly-looking hens. The air was so filled with turf-smoke that we went out again in a moment into the open air. As we were standing about we heard the carman asking the boy why he was not at school.

'I'm spreading turf this day,' he said, 'and my brother is at school. To-morrow he'll stay at home, and it will be my turn to go.'

Then an old man came up and spoke of the harm the new potato crop is getting from the high wind, as indeed we had seen ourselves in several fields that we had passed, where the whole lines of the tops were broken and withered.

'There was a storm like this three weeks ago,' he said, 'and I could hardly keep my old bonnet on me going round through the hills. This storm is as bad, or near it, and wherever there are loops and eddies in the wind you can see the tops all fluttered and destroyed, so that I'm thinking another windy day will leave us as

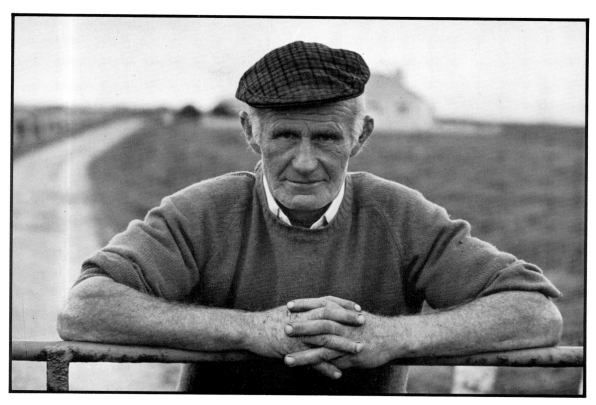

44. Farmer, Belmullet

badly off as we were last year.'

It seems that about here the damage of the sea-winds, where there is no shelter, does as much or more harm than the blight itself. Still the blight is always a danger, and for several years past the people have been spraying their crops, with sufficiently good results to make them all anxious to try it. Even an old woman who could not afford to get one of the machines used for this purpose was seen out in her field a season or two ago with a bucketful of the solution, spraying her potatoes with an old broom — an instance which shows how eager the people are to adopt any improved methods that can be shown to be of real value. This took place in the neighbourhood of Aghoos — the place we were driving to — where an estate has been bought by the Congested Districts Board and resold to the tenants. The holdings are so small that the rents are usually about three pounds a year, though in some cases they are much less, and it is easily seen that the people must remain for a while at least as poor, or nearly as poor, as they have been in the past. In barren places of this kind the enlarging of the holdings is a matter of the greatest difficulty, as good land is not to be had in the neighbourhood; and it is hard to induce even a few families to migrate to another place where holdings could be provided for them, while their absence would liberate part of the land in a district that is overcrowded. At present most of the holdings have, besides their tilled land, a stripe of rough bog-land, which is to be gradually reclaimed; but even when this is done the holdings will remain poor and small, and if a bad season comes the people may be again in need of relief. Still no one can deny the good that is done by making the tenants masters of their own ground and consolidating their holdings, and when the old fear of improvements, caused by the landlord system, is thoroughly forgotten, something may be done.

A great deal has been said of the curse of the absentee landlord; but in reality the small landlord, who lived on his property, and knew how much money every tenant possessed, was a far greater evil. The judicial rent system was not a great deal better, as when the term came to an end the careless tenant had his rent lowered, while the man who had improved his holding remained as he was — a fact which, of course, meant much more than the absolute value of the money lost. For one reason or another, the reduction of rents has come to be, in the tenants' view, the all-important matter; so that this system kept down the level of comfort, as every tenant was anxious to appear as poor as possible for fear of giving the landlord an advantage. These matters are well known; but at the present time the state of suspended land-purchase is tending to reproduce the same fear in a new form, and any tenants who have not bought out are naturally afraid to increase the price they may have to pay by improving their land. In this district, however, there is no fear of this kind, and a good many small grants have been given by the Board for rebuilding cottages and other improvements. A new cottage can be built by the occupier himself for a sum of about thirty pounds, of which the Board pays only a small part, while cottages built by the Board on their own plan, with slated roofs on them, cost double, or more than double, as much. We went into one of the re-slated cottages with concrete floors, and it was curious to see that, however awkward the building looked from the outside, in the kitchen itself the stain of the turf-smoke and the old pot-ovens and stools made the place seem natural and local. That at least was reassuring.

45. *Waiting for the Dole, Binghamstown*

ERRIS

IN THE poorest districts of Connemara the people live, as I have already pointed out, by various industries, such as fishing, turf-cutting, and kelp-making, which are independent of their farms, and are so precarious that many families are only kept from pauperism by the money that is sent home to them by daughters or sisters who are now servant-girls in New York. Here in the congested districts of Mayo the land is still utterly insufficient — held at least in small plots, as it is now — as a means of life, and the people get the more considerable part of their funds by their work on the English or Scotch harvest, to which I have alluded before. A few days ago a special steamer went from Achill Island to Glasgow with five hundred of these labourers, most of them girls and young boys. From Glasgow they spread through the country in small bands and work together under a ganger, picking potatoes or weeding turnips, and sleeping for the most part in barns and outhouses. Their wages vary from a shilling a day to perhaps double as much in places where there is more demand for their work. The men go more often to the north of England, and usually work together, where it is possible, on small contracts for piecework arranged by one of themselves until the hay harvest begins, when they work by the day. In both cases they get fairly good wages, so that if they are careful and stay for some months they can bring back eight or nine pounds with them.

This morning people were passing through the town square of Belmullet — where our windows look out — towards the steamer, from two o'clock, in small bands of boys and girls, many of them carrying their boots under their arms and walking in bare feet, a fashion to which they are more used. Last night also, on our way back from a village that is largely inhabited by harvest people, we saw many similar bands hurrying in towards the town, as the steamer was to sail soon after dawn. This part of the coast is cut into by a great number of shallow tidal estuaries which are dry at low tide, while at full tide one sees many small roads that seem to run down aimlessly into the sea, till one notices, perhaps half a mile away, a similar road running down on the opposite headland. On our way, as the tide was out, we passed one of these sandy fords where there were a number of girls gathering cockles, and drove into Geesala, where we left our car and walked on to the villages of Dooyork, which lie on a sort of headland cut off on the south by another long estuary. It is in places like this, where there is no thoroughfare in any direction to bring strangers to the country, that one meets with the most individual local life. There are two villages of Dooyork, an upper and lower, and as soon as we got into the first every doorway was filled with women and children looking after us with astonishment. All the houses were quite untouched by improvements, and a few of them were broken-down hovels of the worst kind. On the road there were several women bringing in turf or seaweed on horses with large panniers slung over a straw straddle, on which usually a baby of two or three years old was riding with delight. At the end of the village we talked to a man who had been in America, and before that had often gone to England as a harvestman.

'Some of the men get a nice bit of money,' he said, 'but it is hard work. They begin at three in the morning, and they work on till ten at night. A man will some-times get twelve shillings an acre for hoeing turnips, and a skilful man will do an acre or the better part of it in one day; but I'm telling you it is hard work, and before the day is done a man will be hard set to know if it's the soil or the turnips he's striking down on.'

I asked him where and how they lodged.

'Ah,' he said, 'don't ask me to speak to you of that, for the lodging is poor, surely.'

We went on then to the next village, a still more primitive and curious one. The houses were built close together, with passages between them, and low, square yards marked round with stones. At one corner we came on a group of dark brown asses with panniers, and women standing among them in red dresses, with white or coloured handkerchiefs over their heads; and the whole scene had a strangely foreign, almost Eastern, look, though in its own way it was peculiarly characteristic of Ireland. Afterwards we went back to Geesala, along the edge of the sea. This district has, unexpectedly enough, a strong branch of the Gaelic League, and small Irish plays are acted frequently in the winter, while there is also an Agricultural Co-operative Bank, which has done excellent work. These banks, on the Raiffeisen system, have been promoted in Ireland for the last nine or ten years by the Irish Agricultural Society, with aid from the Congested Districts Board, and in a small way they have done much good, and shown — to those who wished to question it — the business intelligence of the smallest tenant-farmers. The interest made by these local associations tends to check emigration, but in this district the distress of last year has a bad effect. In the last few months a certain number of men have sold out the tenant-right of their holdings — usually to the local shopkeeper, to whom they are always in debt — and shipped themselves and their whole families to America with what remained of the money. This is probably the worst kind of emigration, and one fears the sufferings of these families, who are suddenly moved to such different surroundings, must be great.

This district of the Erris Union, which we have now been through, is the poorest in the whole of Ireland, and during the last few months six or seven hundred people have been engaged on the relief works. Still, putting aside exceptionally bad years, there is certainly a tendency towards improvement. The steamer from Sligo, which has only been running for a few years, has done much good by bringing in flour and meal much more cheaply than could be done formerly. Typhus is less frequent than it used to be, probably because the houses and holdings are improving gradually, and we have heard it said the work done in Aghoos by the fund raised by the *Manchester Guardian* some years ago was the beginning of this better state of things. The relief system, as it is now carried on, is an utterly degrading one, and many things will have to be done before the district is in anything like a satisfactory state. Yet the impression one gets of the whole life is not a gloomy one. Last night was St. John's Eve, and bonfires — a relic of Druidical rites — were lighted all over the country, the largest of all being placed in the town square of Belmullet, where a crowd of small boys shrieked and cheered and threw up firebrands for hours together. To-day, again, there was a large market in the square, where a number of country people, with their horses and donkeys, stood about bargaining for young pigs, heather brooms, homespun flannels, second-hand clothing, blacking-brushes, tinkers' goods and many other articles. Once when I looked out the blacking-brush man and the card-trick man were getting up a fight in the corner of the square. A little later there was another stir, and I saw a China-man wandering about, followed by a wondering crowd. The sea in Erris, as in Connemara, and the continual arrival of islanders and boatmen from various directions, tend to keep up an interest and movement that is felt even far away in the villages among the hills.

THE INNER LANDS OF MAYO
THE VILLAGE SHOP

THERE IS a curious change in the appearance of the country when one moves inland from the coast districts of Mayo to the congested portion of the inner edge of the county. In this place there are no longer the Erris tracts of bog or the tracts of stone of Connemara; but one sees everywhere low hills and small farms of poor land that is half turf-bog, already much cut away, and half narrow plots of grass or tillage. Here and there one meets with little villages, built on the old system, with cottages closely grouped together and filled with primitive people, the women mostly in bare feet, with white handkerchiefs over their heads. On the whole, however, one soon feels that this neighbourhood is far less destitute than those we have been in hitherto. Turning out of Swinford, soon after our arrival, we were met almost at once by a country funeral coming towards the town, with a large crowd, mostly of women, walking after it. The coffin was tied on one side of an outside car, and two old women, probably the chief mourners, were sitting on the other side. In the crowd itself we could see a few men leading horses or bicycles, and several young women who seemed by their dress to be returned Americans. When the funeral was out of sight we walked on for a few miles, and then turned into one of the wayside public-houses, at the same time general shop and bar, which are a peculiar feature of most of the country parts of Ireland. An old one-eyed man, with a sky-blue handkerchief round his neck, was standing at the counter making up his bill with the publican, and disputing loudly over it. Here, as in most of the congested districts, the shops are run on a vague system of credit that is not satisfactory, though one does not see at once what other method could be found to take its place. After the sale of whatever the summer season has produced — pigs, cattle, kelp, etc. — the bills are paid off, more or less fully, and all the ready money of a family is thus run away with. Then about Christmas time a new bill is begun, which runs on till the following autumn — or later in the harvesting districts — and quite small shopkeepers often put out relatively large sums in this way. The people keep no pass-books, so they have no check on the traders, and although direct fraud is probably rare it is likely that the prices charged are often exorbitant. What is worse, the shop-keeper in out-of-the-way places is usually the only buyer to be had for a number of home products, such as eggs, chickens, carragheen moss, and sometimes even kelp; so that he can control the prices both of what he buys and what he sells, while as a creditor he has an authority that makes bargaining impossible : another of the many complicated causes that keep people near to pauperism! Mean-

144

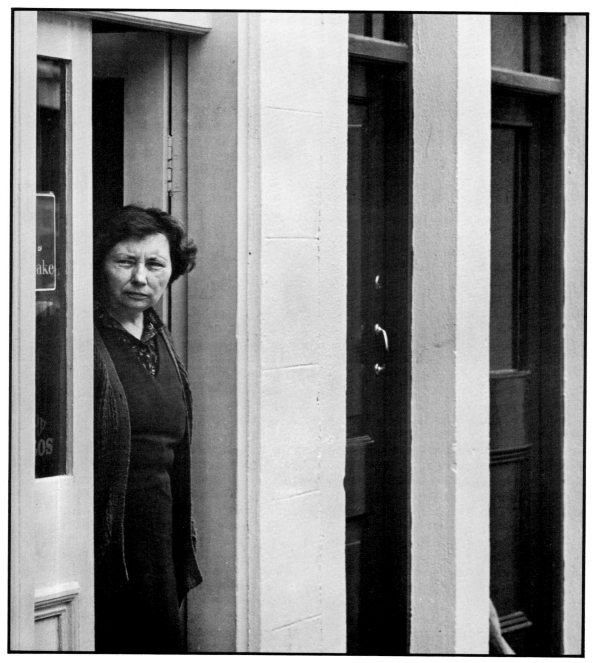

46. *Charlestown*

while the old man's bill was made out, and the publican came to serve us. While he did so the old man spoke to us about the funeral, and I asked him about the returned Americans we had seen going after it.

'All the girls in this place,' he said, 'are going out to America when they are about seventeen years old. Then they work there for six years or more, till they do grow weary of that fixed kind of life, with the early rising and the working late, and then they do come home with a little stocking of fortune with them and they do be tempting the boys with their chains and their rings, till they get a husband and settle down in this place. Such a lot of them is coming now there is hardly a marriage made in the place that the women hasn't been in America.'

I asked a woman who had come in for a moment if she thought the girls kept their health in America.

'Many of them don't,' she said, 'working in factories with dirty air; and then you have likely seen that the girls in this place is big, stout people, and when they get over beyond they think they should be in the fashions, and they begin squeezing themselves in till you hear them gasping for breath, and that's no healthy way to be living.'

When we offered the old man a drink a moment later, he asked for twopenny ale.

'This is the only place in Ireland,' he said, 'where you'll see people drinking ale, for it is from this place that the greatest multitudes go harvesting to England — it's the only way they can live — and they bring the taste for ale back along with them. You'll see a power of them that come home at Michaelmas or Martinmas itself that will never do a hand's turn the rest of the year; but they will be sitting around in each other's houses playing cards through the night, and a barrel of ale set up among them.'

I asked him if he could tell about how many went from Swinford and the country round in each year.

'Well,' he said, 'you'd never reckon them, but I've heard people to say that there are six thousand or near it. Trains full of them do be running every week to the city of Dublin for the Liverpool boat, and I'm telling you it's many are hard set to get a seat in them at all. Then if the weather is too good beyond and the hay is near saved of itself, there is some that get little to do; but if the Lord God sends showers and rain there is work and plenty, and a power of money to be made.'

While he was talking some men who were driving cattle from a fair came in and sat about in the shop, drinking neat glasses of whisky. They called for their drinks so rapidly that the publican called in a little barefooted girl in a green dress, who stood on a box beside a porter barrel rinsing glasses while he served the men. They all appeared to know the old man with one eye, and they talked to him about some job he had been doing on the relief works in this district. Then they made him tell a story for us of a morning when he had killed three wild ducks 'with one skelp of a little gun he had,' and the man who was sitting on a barrel at my side told me that the old man had been the best shot in the place till he got too fond of porter, and had had his gun and his licence taken from him because he was shooting wild over the roads. Afterwards they began to make fun of him because his wife had run away from him and gone over the water, and he began to lose his temper. On our way back an old man who was driving an ass with heavy panniers of turf told us

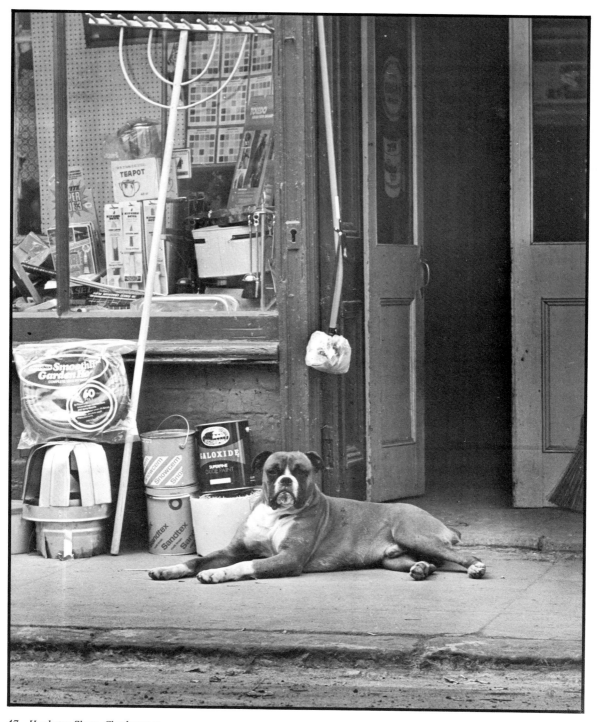

47. Huckster Shop, Charlestown

that all the turf of this district will be cut away in the next twenty years, and the people will be left without fuel. This is taking place in many parts of Ireland, and unless the Department of Agriculture, or the Congested Districts Board, can take steps to provide plantations for these districts there may be considerable suffering, as it is not likely that the people even then will be able to buy coal. Something has been done and a great deal has been said on the subject of growing timber in Ireland, but so far there has been little result. An attempt was made to establish an extensive plantation near Carna, in Connemara, first by the Irish Government in 1890, and then by the Congested Districts Board since 1902; but the work has been a complete failure. Efforts have been made on a smaller scale to encourage planting among the people, but I have not seen much good come of them. Some turf tracts in Ireland are still of great extent, but they are not inexhaustible, and even if turf has to be brought from them, in a few years, to cottagers great distances away, the cost of it will be a serious and additional hardship for the people of many poor localities.

THE SMALL TOWN

MANY OF THE smaller towns of the west and south of Ireland — the towns chiefly that are in or near the congested districts — have a peculiar character. If one goes into Swinford or Charlestown, for instance, one sees a large dirty street strewn in every direction with loose stones, paper, and straw, and edged on both sides by a long line of deserted-looking shops, with a few asses with panniers of turf standing about in front of them. These buildings are mostly two or three storeys high, with smooth slate roofs, and they show little trace of the older sort of construction that was common in Ireland, although there are often a few tiny and miserable cottages at the ends of the town that have been left standing from an older period. Nearly all towns of this class are merely trading centres kept up by the country people that live round them, and they usually stand where several main roads come together from large, out-of-the-way districts. In Swinford, which may be taken as a good example of these market towns, there are seven roads leading into the country, and it is likely that a fair was started here at first, and that the town as it is now grew up afterwards. Although there is at present a population of something over 1,300 people, and a considerable trade, the place is still too small to have much genuine life, and the streets look empty and miserable till a market-day arrives. Then, early in the morning, old men and women, with a few younger women of about thirty who have been in America, crowd into the town and range themselves with their asses and carts at both sides of the road, among the piles of goods which the shopkeepers spread out before their doors.

The life and peculiarities of the neighbourhood — the harvesting and the potato blight, for instance — are made curiously apparent by the selection of these articles. Over nearly every shop door we could see, as we wandered through the town, two scythe-blades fixed at right angles over the doorways, with the points and edges uppermost, and in the street below them there were numbers of hay-rakes standing in barrels, scythe-handles, scythe-blades bound in straw rope, reaping-hooks, scythe-stones, and other things of the kind. In a smith's forge at the end of the town we found a smith fixing blades and hand-grips to scythe-handles for a crowd of men who stood round him with the blades and handles, which they had bought elsewhere, ready in their hands. In front of many shops also one could see old farmers bargaining eagerly for second-hand spraying machines, or buying supplies of the blue sulphate of copper that was displayed in open sacks all down the street. In other places large packing-cases were set up, with small trunks on top of them, and pasted over with advertisements of the various Atlantic lines that are used by emigrants, and large pictures of the Oceanic and other vessels. Inside many of the shops and in the windows one could see an extraordinary collection of objects — saddles, fiddles, rosaries, rat-traps, the Shorter Catechism, castor-oil, rings, razors, rhyme-books, fashion plates, nit-killer, and fine-tooth combs. Other houses had the more usual articles of farm and household use, but nearly all of them, even drapers' establishments, with stays and ribbons in the windows, had a licensed bar at the end, where one could see a few old men or women drinking whisky or beer. In the streets themselves there was a pig-market going on at the upper end of the town near the courthouse, and in another place a sale of barrels and churns, made apparently by a local cooper, and also of many-sized wooden bowls, pig-troughs, and the wooden bars and pegs that are used on donkeys' saddles to carry the panniers. Further down there were a number of new panniers set out, with long bundles of willow boughs set up beside them, and offered for sale by old women and children. As the day went on six or seven old-clothes brokers did a noisy trade from three large booths set up in the street. A few of the things sold were new, but most of them were more or less worn out, and the sale was carried on as a sort of auction, an old man holding up each article in turn and asking first, perhaps, two shillings for a greasy blouse, then cutting away the price to sixpence or even fourpence-halfpenny. Near the booths a number of strolling singers and acrobats were lounging about, and starting off now and then to sing or do contortions in some part of the town. A couple of these men began to give a performance near a booth where we were listening to the bargaining and the fantastic talk of the brokers. First one of them, in a yellow and green jersey, stood on his hands and did a few feats; then he went round with his hat and sold ballads, while the other man sang a song to a banjo about a girl:

> . . . whose name it was, I don't know,
> And she passed her life in a barber's shop
> Making wigs out of sawdust and snow.

Not far away another man set up a stall, with tremendous shouting, to sell some little packets, and we could hear him calling out, 'There's envelopes, notepaper, a pair of boot-laces, a corn-cure for one penny. Take notice, gentlemen.'

All the time the braying of the asses that were standing about the town was incessant and extraordinarily noisy, as sometimes four or five of them took it up at the same time. Many of these asses were of a long-legged, gawky type, quite unusual in this country, and due, we were told, to a Spanish ass sent here by the Congested Districts Board to improve the breed. It is unfortunate that most attempts to

149

improve the live stock of Ireland have been made by some off-hand introduction of a foreign type which often turns out little suited to the new conditions it is brought to, instead of by the slower and less exciting method of improving the different types by selection from the local breeds. We have heard a great deal in passing through Connemara of the harm that has been done by injudicious 'improving' of the ponies and horses, and while it is probable that some of the objections made to the new types may be due to local prejudice, it should not be forgotten that the small farmer is not a fool, and that he knows perfectly well when he has an animal that is suited to his needs.

Towards evening, when the market was beginning to break up, an outside car drove through the town, laden on one side with an immense American trunk belonging to a woman who had just come home after the usual period of six years that she had spent making her fortune. A man at a shop door who saw it passing began to talk about his own time in New York, and told us how often he had had to go down to Coney Island at night to 'recoup' himself after the heat of the day. It is not too much to say that one can hardly spend an hour in one of these Mayo crowds without being reminded in some way of the drain of people that has been and is still running from Ireland. It is, however, satisfactory to note that in this neighbourhood and west of it, on the Dillon estate, which has been bought out and sold to the tenants by the Congested Districts Board, there is a current of returning people that may do much good. A day or two ago we happened to ask for tea in a cottage which was occupied by a woman in a new American blouse, who had unmistakably come home recently from the States. Her cottage was perfectly clean and yet had lost none of the peculiar local character of these cottages. Almost the only difference that one could point to was a large photograph of the head of the Sistine Madonna, hanging over the fire in the little room where we sat, instead of the hideous German oleographs on religious subjects that are brought round by pedlars, and bought by most of the simpler Irish women for the sake of the subjects they represent.

POSSIBLE REMEDIES

IT IS not easy to improve the state of the people in the congested districts by any particular remedy or set of remedies. As we have seen, these people are dependent for their livelihood on various industries, such as fishing, kelp-making, turf-cutting, or harvesting in England; and yet the failure of a few small plots of potatoes brings them literally to a state of famine. Near Belmullet, during a day of storm, we saw the crop for next year in danger of utter ruin, and if the weather had not changed, by good luck, before much harm was done, the whole demoralizing and wretched business of the relief works would have had to be taken up again in a few months. It is obvious that the earnings of the people should be large enough to make them more or less independent of one particular crop, and yet, in reality, it is not easy to

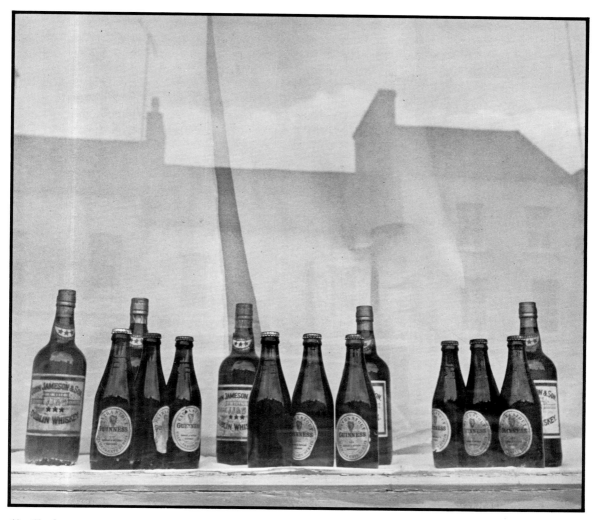

48. *Charlestown*

bring about such a state of things; for the moment a man earns a few extra pounds in a year he finds many good and bad ways of spending them, so that when a quarter of his income is cut away unexpectedly once in seven or eight years he is as badly off as before. To make the matter worse, the pig trade — which is often relied on to bring in the rent-money — is, as I have shown, dependent on the potatoes, so that a bad potato season means a dearth of food, as well as a business difficulty which may have many consequences. It is possible that by giving more attention to the supply of new seed potatoes and good manure — something in this direction is being done by the co-operative societies — the failure of the crop may be made less frequent. Yet there is little prospect of getting rid of the danger altogether, and as long as it continues the people will have many hardships.

The most one can do for the moment is to improve their condition and solvency in other ways, and for this purpose extended purchase on the lines adopted by the Congested Districts Board seems absolutely necessary. This will need more funds than the Board has now at its disposal, and probably some quicker mode of work. Perhaps in places where relief has to be given some force may have to be brought to bear on landlords who refuse to sell at fair terms. No amount of purchase in the poorer places will make the people prosperous — even if the holdings are considerably enlarged — yet there is no sort of doubt that in all the estates which the Board has arranged and sold to the tenants there has been a steady tendency towards improvement. A good deal may be done also by improved communications, either by railroad or by sea, to make life easier for the people. For instance, before the steamer was put on a few years ago between Sligo and Belmullet, the cost of bringing a ton of meal or flour by road from Ballina to Belmullet was one pound, and one can easily estimate the consequent dearness of food. That is perhaps an extreme case, yet there are still a good many places where things are almost as bad, and in these places the people suffer doubly, as they are usually in the hands of one or two small shopkeepers, who can dictate the price of eggs and other small articles which they bring in to sell. At present a steamer running between Westport and Belmullet, in addition to the Sligo boat, is badly needed, and would probably do a great deal of good more cheaply than the same service could be done by a line of railway. If the communications to the poorest districts could be once made fairly satisfactory it would be much easier for the Congested Districts Board, or some similar body, to encourage the local industries of the people and to enable them to get the full market value for what they produce.

The cottage industries that have been introduced or encouraged by the Board — lace-making, knitting, and the like — have done something; yet at best they are a small affair. In a few places the fishing industry has been most successfully developed, but in others it has practically failed, and led to a good deal of disappointment and wasted energy. In all these works it needs care and tact to induce the people to undertake new methods of work; but the talk sometimes heard of their sloth and ignorance has not much foundation. The people have traditional views and instincts about agriculture and live stock, and they have a perfectly natural slowness to adopt the advice of an official expert who knows nothing of the peculiar conditions of their native place. The advice given is often excellent, but there have been a sufficient number of failures in the work done by the Congested

49. After Mass, Louisburgh

153

Districts Board, such as the attempt at forestry in Carna and the bad results got on certain of their example plots laid out to demonstrate the best methods of farming, to make the conservatism of the people a sign of, perhaps, valuable prudence. The Board and the Department of Agriculture and Technical Education have done much excellent work, and it is not to be expected that improvements of this kind, which must be largely experimental, can be carried on without failures; yet one does not always pardon a sort of contempt for the local views of the people which seems rooted in nearly all the official workers one meets with through the country.

One of the chief problems that one has to deal with in Ireland is, of course, the emigration that I have mentioned so often. It is probably the most complicated of all Irish affairs, and in dealing with it it is important to remember that the whole moral and economic condition of Ireland has been brought into a diseased state by prolonged misgovernment and many misfortunes, so that at the present time normal remedies produce abnormal results. For instance, if it is observed in some neighbourhood that the girls are going to America because they have no work at home, and a lace school is started to help them, it too often happens that the girls merely use it as a means of earning money enough to pay for their passage and outfit, and the evil is apparently increased. Further, it should not be forgotten that emigrants are going out at the present time for quite opposite reasons. In the poorest districts of all they go reluctantly, because they are unable to keep themselves at home; but in places where there has been much improvement the younger and brighter men and girls get ambitions which they cannot satisfy in this country, and so they go also. Again, where there is no local life or amusement they go because they are dull, and when amusements and races are introduced they get the taste for amusements, and go because they cannot get enough of them. They go as much from districts where the political life has been allowed to stagnate as from districts where there has been an excess of agitation that has ended only in disappointment. For the present the Gaelic League is probably doing more than any other movement to check this terrible evil, and yet one fears that when the people realise in five, or perhaps in ten, years that this hope of restoring a lost language is a vain one the last result will be a new kind of hopelessness and many crowded ships leaving Queenstown and Galway. Happily in some places there is a counter-current of people returning from America. Yet they are not very numerous, and one feels that the only real remedy for emigration is the restoration of some national life to the people. It is this conviction that makes most Irish politicians scorn all merely economic or agricultural reforms, for if Home Rule would not of itself make a national life it would do more to make such a life possible than half a million creameries. With renewed life in the country many changes of the methods of government, and the holding of property, would inevitably take place, which would all tend to make life less difficult even in bad years and in the worst districts of Mayo and Connemara.

50. Belmullet

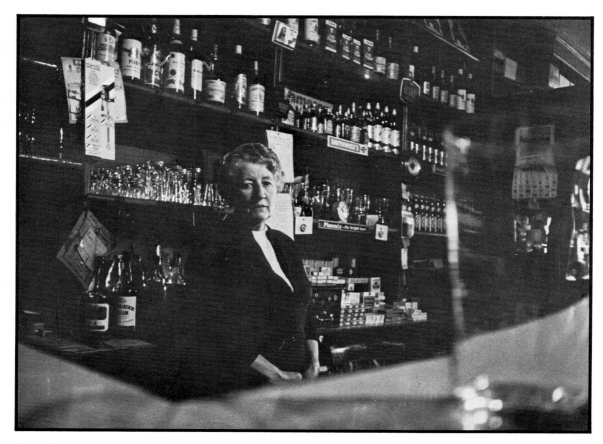

51. Publican-shopkeeper, Cahirciveen

Captions

1   GREAT BLASKET ISLAND *(page 2)*
Blackfaced Mountain Sheep can subsist on the poorest land, nibbling the rocks and rearing their lambs on the bog. They are found all over the hillsides of the south and west of Ireland. They are less inclined to move in flocks than other breeds and can be seen scattered in small clusters over the hills.

2   JUG AND HAND-BASIN *(page 5)*
The deep set window of this traditional cottage provides a convenient resting place for a water jug and hand-basin. Piped water and sinks have replaced the jug and basin in most homes, but in remote areas the journey to the well is still a daily chore. This window shows the thick wall construction of rough stone and mortar often used in smallholders' cottages.

3   NAOMHOG, DUNQUIN (page 6)
Overturned naviogues show their tarred bottoms on the pier below Dunquin. Most are owned by re-located Blasket Island fishermen now living in Dunquin. A recent innovation has been the adoption of small outboard engines. The opening through which the engine protrudes is seen in the bottoms of two boats. While boats of this type are of considerable antiquity on the west coast of Ireland, none were recorded in the Dingle area until the mid 1850s. The road down to the pier which is carved into the cliff must be one of the steepest in Ireland.

4   AVONMORE RIVER *(page 30)*
This beautiful old stone bridge crosses the Avonmore River near Laragh. It flows through a typical Wicklow valley and joins the Avonbeg at the "Meeting of the Waters", a place made famous by Thomas Moore in his song: "There is not in this wide world a valley so sweet as that vale in whose bosom the bright waters meet."

5   TRAVELLING FAMILY *(page 33)*
The nomadic life so admired and often praised by Synge has been shown by social scientists in recent years to be a life of hardship and not necessarily one of choice. This picture shows the traditional bender tent, and with the exception of the modern clothing and plastic baby bottles, it could have been taken sixty years ago. While this type of makeshift "home" was largely replaced by the barrel-top wagon and more recently by the mobile caravan, it is still used by the poorest travelling families.

6   NEAR KILPEDDER *(page 36)*
Rain falls an average of 199 days per year in County Wicklow and even more frequently in its mountainous areas. Synge believed the rainy weather (actually Wicklow's rainfall is not far off the national average) was a contributing factor in the 'nervous depression' of the Wicklow country people.

7   DEER PARK GLEN, POWERSCOURT *(page 38)*
The sunlit road winds through the Deer Park Glen, a narrow, horse-shoe shaped valley in the Powerscourt demesne. Synge frequently walked in the hills and glens nearby. The 34,000 acre estate developed since 1731 by the Wingfield family served all the needs of the aristocratic land-owning class with its farm, extensive gardens, walks of exotic and rare hardwood trees, freshwater fishing, and deerpark. The great house and estate was sold by Viscount Powerscourt to the Slazenger family in recent years.

8   TRAVELLING WOMAN *(page 42)*
"Bred, born and reared" in Wexford, Biddy Connors spent most of her 76 years travelling in Wexford, Wicklow and Carlow. For the past 13 years she has lived on the outskirts of Dublin surrounded by family including 5 sons and more than 50 of her 98 grandchildren.

9   GLENDALOUGH *(page 44)*
In a short deeply incised valley are some of Ireland's most impressive early monastic remains. Most prominent among the ruins is the round tower standing 103 feet high, with five storeys. The round tower was constructed around the 9th century in response to Viking raids. It served as both a look-out and a place of refuge during an attack. The conical roof fell off many years ago, but was rebuilt with the original stones in 1875.

157

10 POWERSCOURT WATERFALL *(page 47)*
In the Powerscourt demesne run-off from the Wicklow uplands tumbles spectacularly over a cliff to the valley floor over 200 feet below. Near the bottom the waterfall is broken up by angular blocks of granite before re-emerging to form the River Dargle.

11 A TRAVELLING MAN *(page 50)*
In Synge's time, Tinkers travelled by pony and cart or on foot carrying their bag of tools on their backs. It was not until World War I that Ireland's travelling people acquired barrel-top wagons from visiting English Gypsies, fleeing British conscription. At first only the wealthier horse-dealing families could afford wagons, but by the mid-1930s most travelling families owned them. Many built their own simply by adding a hooped superstructure onto an ordinary dray or flat cart. Since the 1960s wagons have been declining in number as Travellers have become motorized, substituting lorry-drawn trailers, for the horse-drawn caravan. This proud Traveller was camped by himself, with only his wife and dogs for company on a quiet lane in the hills. As he explained, I prefer being on me own. The young childer today have gone wild, and you get no peace in a camp."

12 GREAT SUGARLOAF MOUNTAIN *(page 52)*
Wicklow's most prominent landmark is the shapely white cone of the Great Sugar Loaf Mountain (1,654 feet). From the top one can see a variety of landscapes and man's action on them: to the south, a crazy-quilt pattern of farmland, in various shades of yellows and greens; to the west, the rolling barren uplands of the Wicklow hills covered in deep peat bogs, with long scars where men have been at work: to the east, deep wooded gorge of the Glen of the Downs, and still further the greenish-blue waters of the Irish Sea; finally, to the north are the peaks of the Dublin Mountains beyond which lies the vast urban sprawl of Dublin, into which is packed one-third of the nation's population.

13 SERVANTS QUARTERS, POWERSCOURT *(page 54)*
Despite the bad reputation landlords had it must be admitted that they sometimes housed their servants in relatively comfortable quarters. Here is an example in the Powerscourt estate, a stone and brick building constructed around 1840 which housed two families. It was roofed with Blue Bangor slates which because of their value have been removed and used in repairing period houses in Dublin.

14 and 15 GLENCREE *(page 58)*
The village of Glencree nestles at the head of a picturesque valley in the Wicklow Mountains. The large buildings in the centre were one of a series of barracks built by the British along the Military Road after the 1798 rising. In post-colonial times the barracks have been used as a reformatory and as a home for refugee children. The valley itself was once covered by a forest of oak and at one time was preserved by the English sovereign as a royal park.

16 ENNISKERRY *(page 60)*
Young girls cycling through Wicklow stop for a rest in Enniskerry, one of the prettiest villages in Ireland.

17 ROVING SWAN, DINGLE *(page 64)*
Lying on its bottom and carrying about 100 lobster pots is this typical wooden fishing vessel, the *Roving Swan*. In Synge's day fishing was confined to small boats, but in the last fifteen years the Irish government through its *Bord Iascaigh Mhara* (Fisheries Board) has launched a boat and harbour building programme as well as an "eat-more-fish" campaign that has helped many fishing families in the west. Fishing has become an international issue with conflict and tension arising over fishing limits, size of nets, quotas, and the ever present native and foreign poacher.

18 DINGLE PIPER *(page 67)*
Unlike the traditional Irish uileann bagpipe, which is inflated by a bellows strapped to the body, the Scottish highland bagpipe seen here is inflated by the mouth through a blow pipe. A modern version of the itinerant musicians and bards of medieval times, this young Scottish piper supports himself, his drinking and his travels by playing for the public, and whatever change passers-by drop into his hat.

19 DINGLE TOWN *(page 69)*
Dingle, "the most westerly town in Europe", is a small market town and fishing port. In the 1970s

it became a major tourist centre as Continentals and Americans discovered, partially from the film 'Ryan's Daughter', the splendid cliff scenery and rugged mountains west of the town. After a steady decline in popularion from 3,386 in 1841, on the eve of the Famine, to just 1,400 in 1936, the town is now growing again. The heart of Dingle is seen here from the steeple of St. Mary's Church on Green Street. In the distance are the sheltered waters of Dingle Bay.

20   THE BELLRINGER, DINGLE *(page 72)*
One of the responsibilities of the church sacrist is to ascend the circular stone stairs and wooden ladder into the steeple to ring the church bells and notify the community, which is all within earshot, that mass is about to begin. The bells are also rung for the angelus and at appointed times during mass and other services.

21   ST. MARY'S CHURCH, DINGLE *(page 73)*
The russett-coloured Catholic Church in Dingle was built in 1804 from red sandstone quarried in the nearby Slieve Mish mountains, and dolomite limestone. Recently renovated it now has a copper roof.

22   GREAT BLASKET ISLAND *(page 75)*
Great Blasket Island seen through a telephoto lens from the mainland. A central spire runs most of the four mile length of the island, with the land dropping steeply away into magnificent sea cliffs at either side. The first peak was known by the islanders as *Dún* (fort), presumably for the prehistoric settlement nearby. The second peak and the tallest (950 ft.) was called *Cró,* which has various meanings. The former village is seen at the lower left, in a depression which offers some shelter from the strong Atlantic gales which strike the island with tremendous force in winter. The low-lying island in the foreground is Beginish, which was used only for grazing sheep.

23   TEARAUGHT ISLAND *(page 76)*
These Black-faced Mountain Sheep which have not been sheared in three or four years are grazing along a sea cliff on Great Blasket Island. In the distance a submerged mountain with its peak rising sheerly from the Atlantic to a height of 600 ft. forms Tearaught Island, the most westerly in Europe. The beacon on the far side of Tearaught

was the last sign of land Irish emigrants saw on their long voyage to the New World.

24   FISHERMAN, GREAT BLASKET ISLAND *(page 80)*
Two young fishermen along with several others now live on Great Blasket during the summer months. Here a fisherman is returning to shore after tending his lobster pots. The boat is a naviogue. It is constructed of tarred fabric stretched tightly over a wooden frame. While the construction techniques are identical to the currachs of Galway and northward, the naviogue is longer and is tapered at the stern. 'No stern in the world', according to Celtic scholar Robin Flower, 'rides more lightly on the water or answers more readily to the faintest suggestion of the oar'. Its lightness and low draft make it easy to launch from a sandy beach.

25   THE VILLAGE, GT. BLASKET ISLAND *(page 84)*
In 1953 the four remaining households, the last of many generations of Blasket Islanders, were moved off the island due to economic hardship, declining fish catches and the government's difficulty in providing services for such a small population. Today all but four of the original houses are shells, with weeds and ferns growing where the inhabitants once warmed themselves by the open hearth. The building in the foreground was the schoolhouse where up to 40 pupils once learned their lessons in Irish. The roofs were removed in 1954 when many of the islanders returned from their new homes on the mainland to salvage whatever they could. Today many of the timbers can be seen as fence posts around Dunquin. In the 1970s most of the houses were bought from the islanders for a reported £150 each by an American.

26   COUMEENOOLE, DINGLE PENINSULA *(page 87)*
In the small stony fields along the southwestern coast potatoes are planted in 'ridges', known as lazy-beds in some parts of the country, which are shaped by hand with a spade. In this photograph taken in mid-May the new stalks have just come up. The high walls surrounding the small fields were built as much as a means of clearing the field of stones as a barrier to marauding farm animals. This farm perched on the coastal incline in Coumeenoole near Slea Head is typical of the mixed cottage farming so common along the

southwestern seaboard. The farmer in addition to growing potatoes has a few other vegetables, a few chickens, a few milk cows and a flock of sheep which graze on the common land above the village. The two specks of land on the horizon are the Skellig Islands.

27 CAHA MOUNTAINS *(page 89)*
The skull of a wild goat lies on the boggy ground of the Caha Mountains between Glengariff and Kenmare. The wild goat is actually the same as the common domestic goat which is still kept in parts of Ireland for its milk and hides.

28 PUCK FAIR, KILLORGLIN *(page 93)*
Despite the increased importance of modern livestock marts, traditional fairs like Puck Fair in Killorglin still provide a major outlet for stock sales for small farmers in the isolated areas of the country. This Kerry farmer is looking for a buyer for his donkey and her twin foals. However, he will not be consummating the sale of his donkeys with alcohol, as is the custom, for there is a Pioneer pin on his lapel.

29 TIN WHISTLE PLAYER *(page 95)*
Irish traditional music has achieved great popularity in recent years. It is found in many forms, ranging from big groups of singers and musicians who play the fiddle, accordeon, harp, tin whistle, and *bodhrán* (drum) to the unaccompanied singer so familiar to Synge. In this picture a tin whistle soloist plays for his own enjoyment and that of passers-by. The instrument has been made popular by its cheapness, portability, and the great flexibility of tone and mood made possible by a skilled player.

30 VALENTIA ISLAND *(page 99)*
Waves beat against the seaward side of Valentia Island which takes the full force of the Atlantic swell. During the 17th and 18th centuries, Valentia's sheltered harbour became a famous smuggling port for French and American privateers, including John Paul Jones. In the last century Valentia became the eastern terminal station for the first transatlantic cable. The first cable messages were received on August 16, 1858.

31 BEARA PENINSULA *(page 102)*
This photograph shows the bay, peninsula and offshore islands near Ardgroom, looking northward towards the Iveragh peninsula. Although the silhouetted structure in the foreground appears to have been a big house, it is too near the water's edge, and was probably a coastguard station. The numerous islands and shallow waters which prevented ships of war from pursuing small boats made this area a smugglers paradise, and hence the presence of the coastguard.

32 GREEN STREET, DINGLE *(page 105)*
Many families still draw upon a variety of sources for their income. Here, vegetables, furniture, and a pony and cart are sold from a Dingle window.

33 TRALEE MARKET *(page 105)*
The small outdoor fruit and vegetable market is still popular in many Irish towns and cities. Shopping is more personal and, with cheaper prices than in the foodstores, outdoor trading is likely to continue in the future. Compared to markets in other parts of Europe the range of fruits and vegetables for sale is quite limited.

34 CAHIRCIVEEN *(page 108)*
In the past many of the country's poor kept a flock of geese, since geese are able to find their own food and are easy to care for. Up to the 1940s it was the goose that provided the Christmas dinner; the turkey being a post-War innovation. The geese here are feeding alongside ruins on a back street in Cahirciveen.

35 BLASKET ISLANDS *(page 110)*
The roads in this part of Kerry provide unexpected and dramatic changes of scene with each bend. Here the Blasket Islands appear hazy and small on a calm but cloudy spring day. There is a speed boat service to the main island during the summer, which seems to ignore the strong currents that meant danger and isolation to the islanders of Synge's time.

36 CARRAROE *(page 115)*
In the boulder strewn landscape of coastal Connemara the small plots of arable land are not enough to provide subsistence for some families. Like this man, many of the local inhabitants are both farmers and fishermen.

37 NEAR COSTELLOE *(page 118)*
For centuries in Europe there have been two separate traditions for building plank boats. In the *carvel* technique planks are laid edge to edge to give a smooth hull appearance with caulking used to seal the joints. In *clinker* construction the planks overlap. In carvel the strength and shape of the boat comes from the internal framework, much like in a currach, in the clinker style it comes from the external plank work. These two European boat building traditions have met in Ireland with clinker being common along the east and north-west coasts and carvel found along the west coast from Mayo southwards. Here we find examples of both traditions alongside one another in a small quay in Costelloe.

38 TURF-CUTTING, STH. WEST GALWAY *(page 121)*
Before the turf can be 'won' or dug, the top layer of matted grasses called the 'scraw' must be removed. The turf is then dug with a *sléan,* a long narrow spade with a wing, and spread on the surface to dry. Thrusting the *sléan* into the peat bog is like cutting into an enormous slab of black butter. After the sods have shed some of their water they are piled into small pyramidal 'footings' and later stacked into larger piles, all to assist their drying by the wind. Turf cutting begins in late April or May, when the surface of the bog has dried a bit and the fear of frost has abated — frost pulverizes the sods. In two long days enough turf can be cut for an entire winter's fuel supply.

39 RELIGIOUS STATUES, BALLINROBE *(page 124)*
Religious ikons and pictures are common in Irish homes. In this photograph the Sacred Heart of Jesus and the Immaculate Heart of Mary are silhouetted in a window sill.

40 MULLET PENINSULA *(page 127)*
There are 6.2 million cattle in Ireland — over 2 cattle for every man, woman and child. In many respects pastoralism or animal husbandry, which dates to the earliest inhabitants of the island, has shaped the character of rural Ireland more than agriculture. To this day in the west of Ireland a man measures his land not by the acre but by its grazing capacity, such as 'I have the grass of eight cows'. As Estyn Evans notes, "The countryman would rather have cow dung than soil on his hands . . . . His walk and roving eye are those of the stockmen rather than of the man who drives a plough and keeps his eye on the furrow."

41 FISHERMAN AND LOBSTER POTS, SLASH, BLACKSOD BAY *(page 128)*
Pots constructed of thin laths and net are used to catch lobster and crayfish. Each pot has a stone weight to keep it on the sea floor and a bait attached near the opening to lure the crustacean inside. Once a lobster or crayfish enters the narrow basket-shaped entrance it is trapped inside and cannot crawl out. Most end up on French tables. Here a young fisherman is carrying his pots, four at a time, to his boat on the shores on Blacksod Bay. Because lobster fishing requires working close to cliffs and submerged reefs it is done mainly in the summer months when the seas are calm.

42 LETTERMULLEN ISLAND *(page 132)*
This thatched farmhouse represents the most common vernacular form of architecture found in Ireland. There are three main rooms including a large kitchen-living room in the centre and a bedroom at each end. The design is simple and pleasing to the eye, and its scale and natural colours blend harmoniously with the local surroundings. It is built in a hollow for shelter and probably to make it as inconspicuous as possible; the less often the landlord took notice of a house, the less likely he was to raise the rent. In the foreground is the indispensable patch of potatoes. In the background is more of the boulder-strewn landscape with scanty patches of exposed soil.

43 WEIGH STATION, NEAR BELMULLET *(page 136)*
At this weigh station, two miles outside Belmullet, milk is weighed and inspected for quality. The milk cans are picked up from farmers and transported to the weigh station by 'carriers'. The average farm size in the region is between 15 and 20 acres.

44 FARMER, BELMULLET *(page 139)*
In contrast to the nucleated or clustered form settlements of pre-famine times, the pattern of the Irish country people for the past century has been the lone farm, the isolated holding. This allows the farmer to live close to his livestock, especially milk cows and calves, and thus gives them frequent attention. While most of this man's

161

brothers and sisters emigrated to the big cities of America, particularly Cleveland, he remained to take over the 21 acre family farm. He says the soil is poor, the profits low, and the winters on the western shore of the Mullett peninsula long and miserable, but otherwise feels that he is better off having chosen a life on the land.

45 WAITING FOR THE DOLE, BINGHAMSTOWN *(page 141)*
With much joking and conviviality these Mullet peninsula farmers are waiting on the roadside for the post office to open to collect the dole.

46 CHARLESTOWN *(page 145)*
In small towns everywhere, watching the comings and goings of one's neighbours is a common pastime.

47 HUCKSTER SHOP, CHARLESTOWN *(page 147)*
In the 'huckster' shop, still to be found in many western towns, you can buy anything from a needle to an anchor. Some of the items for sale are still hand-crafted, such as the tinkers' tinware and the handrake made of timber seen here.

48 CHARLESTOWN *(page 151)*
The roofline of this depressed market town is reflected in a pub window, displaying two of Ireland's better known products.

49 AFTER MASS, LOUISBURGH *(page 153)*
The after Mass chat is an old tradition, particularly among the men. Here men dressed in their Sunday best line the footpath to discuss politics and sport and watch the 'town go by'. A member of the younger generation, not yet interested, might someday join them if he does not move to the city or emigrate first.

50 BELMULLET *(page 155)*
Belmullet is one of the most remote towns in Ireland. It is located on the Blacksod Bay on a narrow neck of land which connects the Mullet peninsula with the mainland. After years of decline, the population of this small seaport is now increasing. And so is its prosperity. Its location has been removed to a great extent by motor transport and in recent years by incoming industry including pharmaceutical and electronics firms. The man seated outside his home is contributing, perhaps unwittingly, to an interesting statistic — that Ireland has one of the highest rates of newspaper readership in Western Europe.

51 PUBLICAN-SHOPKEEPER, CAHIRCIVEEN *(page 156)*
The combined general merchant/public house which was once so common in Ireland is disappearing. Many still remain in western Ireland however, such as this example in Cahirciveen (the shop portion is through the door to the left). Though the proprietor believes the general shop will not survive into the next generation as many local people now travel to Tralee to shop. As another shopkeeper explained, 'People have transport now, they have their own cars and they think it's kind of grand to go shopping'. Tralee is a 40 mile drive, 80 miles round-trip.

52 BLASKET ISLAND HOUSE AND BEEHIVE CELL *(page 164)*
This is a typical Blasket Island house, a rectangular shell built of roughly shaped stones mortared with mud, painted with white or yellow lime, and roofed with timber covered with tarred felt. In an earlier time the houses were thatched with rushes which rotted easily and let through a constant drip. The dry-stone structures attached to the far end of the house were an outhouse (left) and a storage (right) for turf, fish and potatoes. Right foreground is an old beehive cell, which was used by the island school teacher to cure and store fish.

Subject Index

Ale 146
Architecture
  Cottages 134, 138
  Towns 148
Asses 149
Asylum (*see* Mental health)

Ballad/ballad-singer 34, 149
Beggarmen (*see* begging)
Begging/beggars 29, 32,
  104, 114, 120
Big Wind, The (1839) 39
Blacksmith 149
Blight, potato (*see also*
  Famine) 140
Bog (*see also* turf cutting)
  37, 134, 135
Boat building 131, 133

Car-drivers 137-8
Carragheen moss, gathering
  of 91
Canoes 109
Circus 68, 70
Climate 35
  Effect on people 35
Cottage industries 152
Conflict/fighting 34
Congested Districts Board
  117, 129, 133, 138, 140,
  148, 149-50, 152, 154
Connemara ponies 117, 150
Curraghs (*see* canoes)
Cures/folk medicine 71, 74

Dance 66, 81, 83
Death - taking your fortune
  with you 88, 90
Department of Agriculture &
  Technical Education 154
Diet 35
Dress 41, 113, 114
Drink/drinking 46, 49, 79,
  82, 101, 146

Education 45, 46

Emigration (*see also* return
  migration) 66, 97, 98, 119,
  143, 146, 154
  Remittances 126, 142

Fairies 31
Famine, The Great 29, 39,
  40, 88, 138
Fiddle 109
Fishing 78, 82
Funeral 144

Gaelic League 143, 154
Garden 55, 56

Home Rule 154
Hooker, Galway Bay 114,
  122
Horse-races 98, 100-101

Isolation/Loneliness 35-37,
  125

Kelp making 126, 129,
  130-131

Labour-migration 142-143,
  146
Lace-school 119, 154
Landed classes 39, 55-56
Landlords (*see* landed classes)
Language 65-66, 107
  Irish 114, 154
  dialects 41, 46
Longevity 29
Loneliness (*see* isolation)
Literacy, attitude towards 66

Match-making 31
Mental health
  Asylum 45
  Nervousness, nerves 37
Music (*see also* songs, dance)
  83, 109

Peelers 103-104
Pig raising 135
Poetry 39
Police 33-34
Poteen 119
Puck Fair 91-97

Racing (*see* horse-racers)
Rearrangements of holdings
  133
Rebellion, The (1798) 46
Relief Works 120-123, 135,
  138, 143
Remittances (*see* emigration)
Return migration/returned
  emigrants 43, 71, 97, 125-
  126, 144-146, 150, 154

St. John's Eve 143
Sea accidents 107
Shops/shopkeepers 144, 149,
  152
Songs 70, 94, 96, 149
Speech (*see* language)
Storytelling 88, 98, 100

Thatch 133
Tinkers 31-2, 37, 43
Tramps (*see* vagrants)
Travel, description and
  conditions of –
  Ballina to Belmullet 134-5
  Blasket Islands 74
  Dingle to Ballydavid 70-1
  Killorglin to Dublin 97-8
  Tralee to Dingle 63-5,
    106-7
Turf cutting (*see also* bogs)
  117, 146, 148
Typhus fever 119, 143

Vagrants 29-35, 37, 60

Weather (*see* climate)
Weaving 85, 137
Witchery/witchcraft 31

163

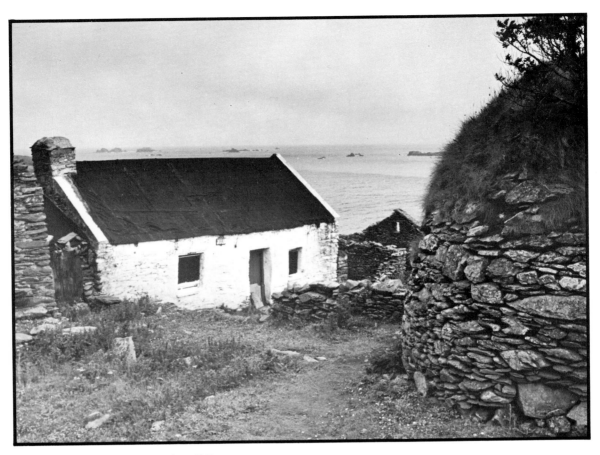

52. *Blasket Island House and Beehive Cell*

Place Index

[00] = illustration

Note: This index is a comprehensive listing of all places mentioned in the text. Some of the places, particularly foreign, are only mentioned in passing. While a shorter listing of only places about which there is some description may seem more useful to the casual reader, a complete listing was decided upon for those interested in the work of J. M. Synge and the various influences upon his writing.